Ninja Dual Zone Air Fryer Cookbook

Quick, Flavorful, Mouthwatering Air Fryer Recipes to Enjoy Delicious and Healthy Meals At Home | including Delicious Breakfast, Snacks, Dinner, ... Desserts & More

Concetta Carlson

All Rights Reserved.

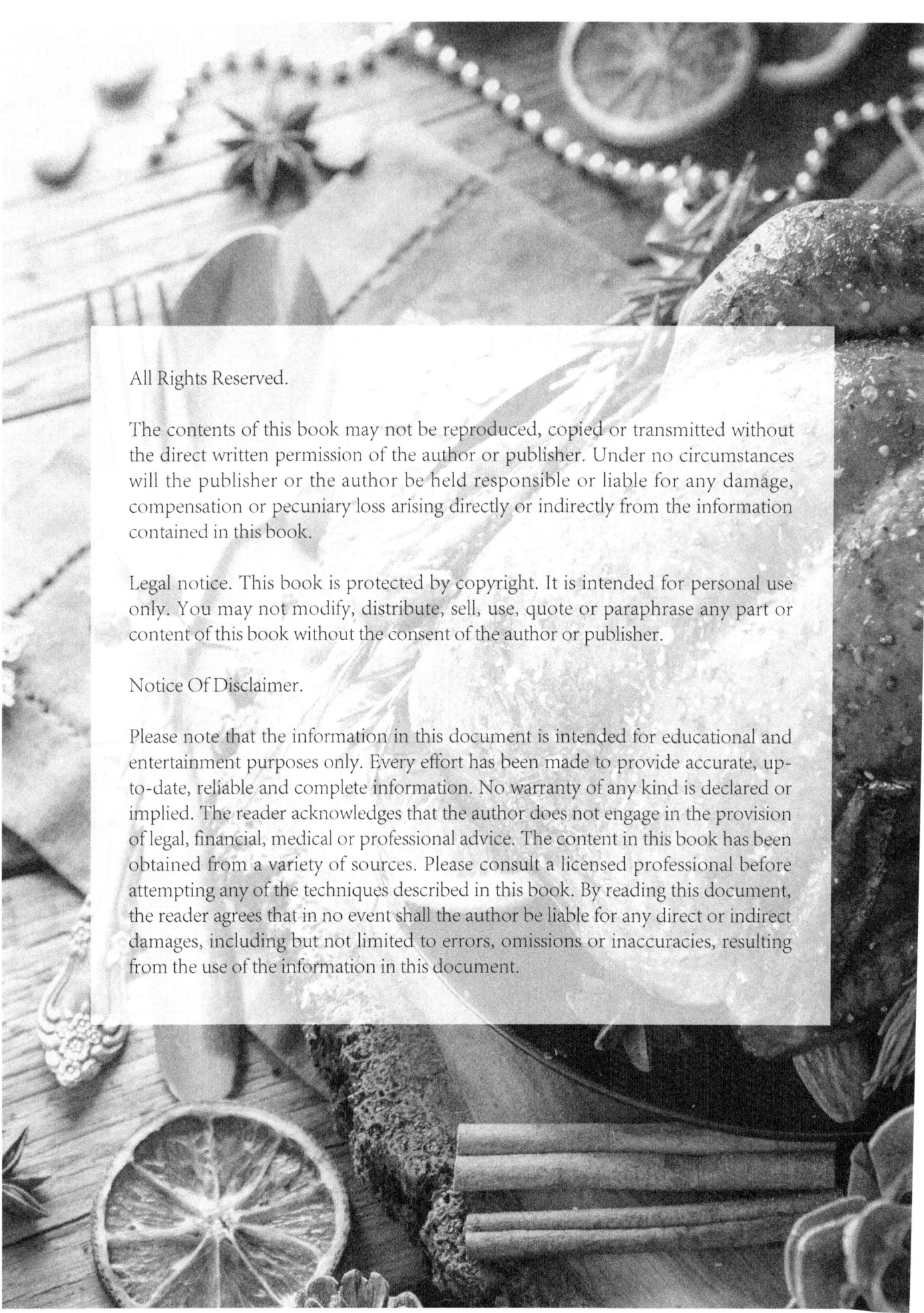

The contents of this book may not be reproduced, copied or transmitted without the direct written permission of the author or publisher. Under no circumstances will the publisher or the author be held responsible or liable for any damage, compensation or pecuniary loss arising directly or indirectly from the information contained in this book.

Legal notice. This book is protected by copyright. It is intended for personal use only. You may not modify, distribute, sell, use, quote or paraphrase any part or content of this book without the consent of the author or publisher.

Notice Of Disclaimer.

Please note that the information in this document is intended for educational and entertainment purposes only. Every effort has been made to provide accurate, up-to-date, reliable and complete information. No warranty of any kind is declared or implied. The reader acknowledges that the author does not engage in the provision of legal, financial, medical or professional advice. The content in this book has been obtained from a variety of sources. Please consult a licensed professional before attempting any of the techniques described in this book. By reading this document, the reader agrees that in no event shall the author be liable for any direct or indirect damages, including but not limited to errors, omissions or inaccuracies, resulting from the use of the information in this document.

CONTENTS

INTRODUCTION 11

BREAD AND BREAKFAST 12

    Meaty Omelet 12

    Brown Sugar Grapefruit 12

    Honey Oatmeal 12

    Seedy Bagels 13

    Mini Everything Bagels 13

    Fancy Cranberry Muffins 14

    French Toast Sticks Recipes 14

    Crispy Samosa Rolls 14

    Orange Trail Oatmeal 15

    Shakshuka-style Pepper Cups 15

    Chocolate Almond Crescent Rolls 16

    Southwest Cornbread 16

    Soft Pretzels 16

    Mediterranean Granola 17

    Baked Eggs 17

    Apple-cinnamon-walnut Muffins 18

    Blueberry Applesauce Oat Cake 18

    Ham & Cheese Sandwiches 18

    Vodka Basil Muffins With Strawberries 19

    Green Egg Quiche 19

APPETIZERS AND SNACKS 20

Blooming Onion 20

Fiery Bacon-wrapped Dates 21

Garlic Wings 21

Chinese-style Potstickers 22

Honey Tater Tots With Bacon 22

Caponata Salsa 22

Apple Rollups 23

Cheesy Spinach Dip(2) 23

Avocado Fries With Quick Salsa Fresca 24

Beef Steak Sliders 24

Garlic Breadsticks 25

Balsamic Grape Dip 25

Arancini With Sun-dried Tomatoes And Mozzarella 25

Spicy Chicken And Pepper Jack Cheese Bites 26

Basil Feta Crostini 26

Crunchy Parmesan Edamame 27

Barbecue Chicken Nachos 27

Cheese Straws 28

Beer Battered Onion Rings 28

Greek Street Tacos 29

POULTRY RECIPES 29

Tortilla Crusted Chicken Breast 29

Spinach And Feta Stuffed Chicken Breasts 30

Buttermilk-fried Drumsticks 30

Restaurant-style Chicken Thighs 31

Honey Lemon Thyme Glazed Cornish Hen 31

Chicken Strips 31

Prosciutto Chicken Rolls 32

Pickle Brined Fried Chicken 32

Kale & Rice Chicken Rolls 33

Indian Chicken Tandoori 33

Ranch Chicken Tortillas 34

Buttery Chicken Legs 34

Chicken Chunks 34

Coconut Chicken With Apricot-ginger Sauce 35

Southwest Gluten-free Turkey Meatloaf 35

Chicken Adobo 36

Crispy Duck With Cherry Sauce 36

Cajun Chicken Livers 37

Christmas Chicken & Roasted Grape Salad 37

Crunchy Chicken Strips 38

BEEF, PORK & LAMB RECIPES 38

Cheeseburger Sliders With Pickle Sauce 38

California Burritos 39

Pork Taco Gorditas 39

Indonesian Pork Satay 40

Crispy Ham And Eggs 40

Balsamic Marinated Rib Eye Steak With Balsamic Fried Cipollini Onions 41

Crispy Pierogi With Kielbasa And Onions 41

Berbere Beef Steaks 42

Fusion Tender Flank Steak 42

Tarragon Pork Tenderloin 42

Wiener Schnitzel 43

Asy Carnitas 43

Delicious Juicy Pork Meatballs 44

Balsamic Beef & Veggie Skewers 44

Tex-mex Beef Carnitas 44

Steak Fajitas 45

Kentucky-style Pork Tenderloin 45

Calf's Liver 45

Horseradish Mustard Pork Chops 46

Cajun Pork Loin Chops 46

FISH AND SEAFOOD RECIPES 47

Hazelnut-crusted Fish 47

Tuna Nuggets In Hoisin Sauce 47

Black Olive & Shrimp Salad 48

Cajun-seasoned Shrimp 48

Sriracha Salmon Melt Sandwiches 48

Fish Piccata With Crispy Potatoes 49

The Best Shrimp Risotto 49

Cheesy Salmon-stuffed Avocados 50

Garlic-butter Lobster Tails 50

Easy Scallops With Lemon Butter 50

Holiday Lobster Salad 51

Almond-crusted Fish 51

Sea Bass With Fruit Salsa 52

Fish Nuggets With Broccoli Dip 52

Beer-breaded Halibut Fish Tacos 52

Kid's Flounder Fingers 53

Masala Fish 'n' Chips 53

Crab Cakes 54

Mediterranean Salmon Cakes 54

Cilantro Sea Bass 54

VEGETARIAN RECIPES 55

Spinach & Brie Frittata 55

Tomato & Squash Stuffed Mushrooms 55

Basic Fried Tofu 56

Quinoa Burgers With Feta Cheese And Dill 56

Roasted Vegetable Stromboli 57

Vegetarian Paella 58

Spinach And Cheese Calzone 58

Harissa Veggie Fries 58

Sesame Orange Tofu With Snow Peas 59

Quinoa & Black Bean Stuffed Peppers 59

Vegetarian Eggplant "pizzas" 60

Easy Zucchini Lasagna Roll-ups 60

Tandoori Paneer Naan Pizza 61

Pinto Taquitos 61

Rainbow Quinoa Patties 62

Zucchini Tamale Pie 62

Tex-mex Potatoes With Avocado Dressing 62

Veggie Fried Rice 63

Spicy Sesame Tempeh Slaw With Peanut Dressing 63

Berbere Eggplant Dip 64

VEGETABLE SIDE DISHES RECIPES 65

Caraway Seed Pretzel Sticks 65

Smoked Avocado Wedges 65

Curried Fruit 65

Sicilian Arancini 66

Shoestring Butternut Squash Fries 66

Truffle Vegetable Croquettes 66

Citrusy Brussels Sprouts 67

Honey-mustard Asparagus Puffs 67

Garlic-parmesan Popcorn 68

Bacon-wrapped Asparagus 68

Cheesy Cauliflower Tart 68

Dijon Roasted Purple Potatoes 69

Okra 69

Smooth & Silky Cauliflower Purée 69

Blistered Tomatoes 70

Parmesan Garlic Fries 70

Toasted Choco-nuts 70

Classic Stuffed Shells 71

Street Corn 71

Southwestern Sweet Potato Wedges 72

SANDWICHES AND BURGERS RECIPES 72

White Bean Veggie Burgers 72

Thanksgiving Turkey Sandwiches 73

Philly Cheesesteak Sandwiches 73

Lamb Burgers 74

Crunchy Falafel Balls 74

Reuben Sandwiches 75

Chicken Spiedies 75

Perfect Burgers 76

Mexican Cheeseburgers 76

Thai-style Pork Sliders 77

Inside Out Cheeseburgers 77

Chicken Saltimbocca Sandwiches 78

Chicken Club Sandwiches 78

Asian Glazed Meatballs 79

Eggplant Parmesan Subs 79

Provolone Stuffed Meatballs 80

Black Bean Veggie Burgers 80

Salmon Burgers 81

Chili Cheese Dogs 82

Chicken Gyros 82

DESSERTS AND SWEETS 83

Carrot Cake With Cream Cheese Icing 83

Vanilla-strawberry Muffins 83

Roasted Pears 84

Nutella® Torte 84

Fall Caramelized Apples 85

Chocolate Cake 85

Cheese & Honey Stuffed Figs 86

Dark Chokolate Cookies 86

Choco-granola Bars With Cranberries 86

Sweet Potato Pie Rolls 87

Dark Chocolate Cream Galette 87

Air-fried Strawberry Hand Tarts 88

Donut Holes 88

Mom's Amaretto Cheesecake 89

Giant Buttery Oatmeal Cookie 89

Molten Chocolate Almond Cakes 90

Vegan Brownie Bites 90

Rustic Berry Layer Cake 91

Banana Fritters 91

Holiday Peppermint Cake 91

INDEX **93**

INTRODUCTION

Would you like to follow a healthy lifestyle but still want to enjoy crispy and delicious food?
Feeling weary of the same old routine when preparing dinner?
Tired of cycling through the same recipes over and over again?

If you answer yes, then this cookbook is for you!

Save Time and Energy
The air fryer is your kitchen's time-saving, energy-efficient wonder. No more waiting for preheating or tending to stovetop dishes for hours. With our cookbook, you'll prepare mouthwatering meals in less than 30 minutes. Enjoy the convenience of quick and efficient cooking while conserving energy.

Rich and delicious recipes
Choose from a wide range of rich and delicious recipes, from appetizers and meats to snacks and desserts. This 'Ninja Dual Zone Air Fryer Cookbook' caters for a wide range of tastes and preferences, as well as helping you to improve your cooking skills to ensure you can create a wide variety of dishes.

Perfect for All Skill Levels
Our cookbook is designed to cater to all skill levels, from beginners to advanced users. Create a diverse array of dishes that will impress your family and friends. Whether it's a casual weeknight dinner or a special celebration, you can count on your air fryer to deliver delicious, crispy results.

Less oil and energy saving
This cookbook is ideal for any kitchen. They offer a healthier way to enjoy your favorite fried foods and provide a convenient cooking solution.

This book covers:
Breakfast recipes: mushrooms, eggs, bacon
Snacks and appetizers: French fries, cheese, sandwiches
Vegetables and side dishes: tomatoes, broccoli, potatoes
Meat recipes: beef, pork, lamb, seafood
Dessert recipes: strawberries, lemons, cakes
And so much more...

This book is recommended for all those who want to use the air fryer in their daily meals.
What are you waiting for, click the "Buy Now" button and make yourself a master of cooking!

Bread And Breakfast

Meaty Omelet

Servings: 4 | Prep Time: 5 Minutes | Cooking Time: 20 Minutes

Ingredients:

- 6 eggs
- 1/2 cup grated Swiss cheese
- 3 breakfast sausages, sliced
- 8 bacon strips, sliced
- Salt and pepper to taste

Directions:

1. Preheat air fryer to 180°C/360°F.
2. In a bowl, beat the eggs and stir in Swiss cheese, sausages and bacon.
3. Transfer the mixture to a baking dish and set in the fryer.
4. Bake for 15 minutes or until golden and crisp.
5. Season and serve.

Variations & Ingredients Tips:

- Add some diced bell peppers, onions or mushrooms to the mix.
- Use cheddar, feta or goat cheese instead of Swiss.
- Serve with salsa, hot sauce or ketchup on the side.

Per Serving: Calories: 370; Total Fat: 29g; Saturated Fat: 12g; Cholesterol: 405mg; Sodium: 670mg; Total Carbs: 1g; Dietary Fiber: 0g; Total Sugars: 1g; Protein: 26g

Brown Sugar Grapefruit

Servings: 2 | Prep Time: 5 Minutes | Cooking Time: 4 Minutes

Ingredients:

- 1 grapefruit
- 2 to 4 teaspoons brown sugar

Directions:

1. Preheat air fryer to 205°C/400°F.
2. Cut grapefruit horizontally in half. Trim bottom so it sits flat.
3. Use a paring knife to cut between flesh and peel, then cut sections free from membranes.
4. Sprinkle 1-2 tsp brown sugar on each half.
5. Set a rack in air fryer basket. Place grapefruit halves cut-side up on rack.
6. Air fry at 205°C/400°F for 4 minutes.
7. Let cool 1 minute before serving.

Variations & Ingredients Tips:

- Try different citrus fruits like oranges or clementines.
- Add a pinch of cinnamon or nutmeg to the brown sugar topping.
- Serve with yogurt or cottage cheese for added protein.

Per Serving: Calories: 80; Total Fat: 0g; Saturated Fat: 0g; Cholesterol: 0mg; Sodium: 0mg; Total Carbs: 21g; Dietary Fiber: 2g; Total Sugars: 18g; Protein: 1g

Honey Oatmeal

Servings: 6 | Prep Time: 5 Minutes | Cooking Time: 35 Minutes

Ingredients:

- 2 cups rolled oats
- 2 cups oat milk
- ¼ cup honey
- ½ cup Greek yogurt
- 1 teaspoon vanilla extract
- ½ teaspoon ground cinnamon
- ¼ teaspoon salt
- 1½ cups diced mango

Directions:

1. Preheat air fryer to 190°C/380°F. Stir together the oats, milk, honey, yogurt, vanilla, cinnamon, and salt in a large bowl until well combined. Fold in ¾ cup of the mango and then pour the mixture into a greased

cake pan. Sprinkle the remaining mango across the top of the oatmeal mixture. Bake in the air fryer for 30 minutes. Leave to set and cool for 5 minutes. Serve and enjoy!

Variations & Ingredients Tips:

- Use almond milk, coconut milk or dairy milk instead of oat milk.
- Swap mango for peaches, berries or diced apples.
- Top with chopped nuts, seeds or a dollop of nut butter for extra protein.

Per Serving: Calories: 293; Total Fat: 5g; Saturated Fat: 1g; Cholesterol: 3mg; Sodium: 142mg; Total Carbs: 55g; Dietary Fiber: 6g; Total Sugars: 25g; Protein: 9g

Seedy Bagels

Servings: 4 | Prep Time: 10 Minutes | Cooking Time: 25 Minutes

Ingredients:

- 1 ¼ cups flour
- 2 tsp baking powder
- ½ tsp salt
- 1 cup plain Greek yogurt
- 1 egg
- 1 tsp water
- 1 tsp poppy seeds
- ½ tsp white sesame seeds
- ½ tsp black sesame seeds
- ½ tsp coriander seeds
- 1 tsp cumin powder
- ½ tsp dried minced onion
- 1 tsp coarse salt

Directions:

1. Preheat air fryer to 150°C/300°F.
2. Mix 1 cup flour, baking powder, salt, and cumin.
3. Stir in yogurt to form a dough. Divide into 4.
4. Roll each into a 15-cm log and form into a bagel shape.
5. Whisk egg and water.
6. Make topping with seeds, onion and salt.
7. Brush bagels with egg wash and coat with topping mix.
8. Air fry 12-15 mins until golden brown.

Variations & Ingredients Tips:

- Use different seeds like flax, chia or everything bagel seasoning.
- Add dried fruit or nuts to the dough.
- Brush with egg white only for a vegan option.

Per Serving: Calories: 288; Total Fat: 5g; Saturated Fat: 1g; Cholesterol: 53mg; Sodium: 1043mg; Total Carbs: 50g; Dietary Fiber: 3g; Total Sugars: 4g; Protein: 11g

Mini Everything Bagels

Servings: 4 | Prep Time: 15 Minutes | Cooking Time: 6 Minutes

Ingredients:

- 1 cup all-purpose flour
- 2 teaspoons baking powder
- ½ teaspoon salt
- 1 cup plain Greek yogurt
- 1 egg, whisked
- 1 teaspoon sesame seeds
- 1 teaspoon dehydrated onions
- ½ teaspoon poppy seeds
- ½ teaspoon garlic powder
- ½ teaspoon sea salt flakes

Directions:

1. In a large bowl, mix together the flour, baking powder, and salt. Make a well in the dough and add in the Greek yogurt. Mix with a spoon until a dough forms.
2. Place the dough onto a heavily floured surface and knead for 3 minutes. You may use up to 1 cup of additional flour as you knead the dough, if necessary.
3. Cut the dough into 8 pieces and roll each piece into a 15-cm, snakelike piece. Touch the ends of each piece together so it closes the circle and forms a bagel shape. Brush the tops of the bagels with the whisked egg.
4. In a small bowl, combine the sesame seeds, dehydrated onions, poppy seeds, garlic powder, and sea salt flakes. Sprinkle the seasoning on top of the bagels.
5. Preheat the air fryer to 180°C/360°F. Using a bench scraper or flat-edged spatula, carefully place the bagels into the air fryer basket. Spray the bagel tops with cooking spray. Air-fry the bagels for 6 minutes or until golden brown. Allow the bread to cool at least 10 minutes before slicing for serving.

Variations & Ingredients Tips:

- Use whole wheat flour for a more nutritious bagel.
- Add dried herbs like rosemary or thyme to the seasoning mix.
- Top with cream cheese or your favorite bagel spread.

Per Serving: Calories: 264; Total Fat: 3.5g; Saturated Fat: 1.1g; Cholesterol: 51mg; Sodium: 609mg; Total Carbohydrates: 44.9g; Dietary Fiber: 1.6g; Total Sugars: 2.8g; Protein: 11.7g

Fancy Cranberry Muffins

Servings: 6 | Prep Time: 10 Minutes | Cooking Time: 30 Minutes

Ingredients:

- 1 cup all-purpose flour
- 2 tablespoons whole wheat flour
- 1 teaspoon baking powder
- ⅛ teaspoon baking soda
- Pinch of salt
- 3 tablespoons sugar
- ½ cup dried cranberries
- 1 egg
- 79 ml buttermilk
- 3 tablespoons butter, melted

Directions:

1. Preheat the air fryer to 175°C/350°F. Sift together all-purpose and whole wheat flours, baking powder, baking soda, and salt into a bowl and stir in the sugar. Add in the cranberries and stir; set aside. Whisk the egg, buttermilk, and melted butter into a bowl until combined. Fold the egg mixture into the flour mixture and stir to combine.
2. Grease 6 silicone muffin cups with baking spray. Fill each muffin cup about 2/3, leaving room at the top for rising. Put the muffin cups in the frying basket and bake 14-18 minutes or until a skewer inserted into the center comes out clean. Set on a wire rack for cooling, then serve.

Variations & Ingredients Tips:

- Use raisins, chopped dates or dried cherries instead of cranberries.
- Add some orange zest and ground cinnamon to the batter for extra aroma.
- Top with a streusel made of flour, brown sugar, butter and chopped nuts.

Per Serving: Calories: 242; Total Fat: 8g; Saturated Fat: 5g; Cholesterol: 43mg; Sodium: 210mg; Total Carbs: 38g; Dietary Fiber: 2g; Total Sugars: 17g; Protein: 5g

French Toast Sticks Recipes

Servings: 4 | Prep Time: 10 Minutes | Cooking Time: 7 Minutes

Ingredients:

- 2 eggs
- 118 ml milk
- ⅛ teaspoon salt
- ½ teaspoon pure vanilla extract
- 177 ml crushed cornflakes
- 6 slices sandwich bread, each slice cut into 4 strips
- oil for misting or cooking spray
- maple syrup or honey

Directions:

1. In a small bowl, beat together eggs, milk, salt, and vanilla.
2. Place crushed cornflakes on a plate or in a shallow dish.
3. Dip bread strips in egg mixture, shake off excess, and roll in cornflake crumbs.
4. Spray both sides of bread strips with oil.
5. Place bread strips in air fryer basket in single layer.
6. Cook at 200°C/390°F for 7 minutes or until they're dark golden brown.
7. Repeat steps 5 and 6 to cook remaining French toast sticks.
8. Serve with maple syrup or honey for dipping.

Variations & Ingredients Tips:

- Use cinnamon raisin bread or banana bread for a flavor twist.
- Crush up frosted flakes, honey nut cheerios or graham crackers for the coating.
- Dust with powdered sugar and cocoa powder for a churro-like treat.

Per Serving: Calories: 264; Total Fat: 7g; Saturated Fat: 2g; Cholesterol: 98mg; Sodium: 474mg; Total Carbs: 40g; Dietary Fiber: 2g; Total Sugars: 8g; Protein: 10g

Crispy Samosa Rolls

Servings: 4 | Prep Time: 20 Minutes | Cooking Time: 30 Minutes

Ingredients:

- ⅔ cup canned peas
- 4 scallions, finely sliced
- 2 cups grated potatoes
- 2 tablespoons lemon juice
- 1 teaspoon ground ginger
- 1 teaspoon curry powder
- 1 teaspoon Garam masala
- ¼ cup chickpea flour
- 1 tablespoon tahini
- 8 rice paper wrappers

Directions:

1. Preheat air fryer to 180°C/350°F.
2. Mix the peas, scallions, potatoes, lemon juice, ginger, curry powder, Garam masala, and chickpea flour in a bowl.
3. In another bowl, whisk tahini and 80 ml of water until combined. Set aside on a plate.
4. Submerge the rice wrappers, one by one, into the tahini mixture until they begin to soften and set aside on a plate.
5. Fill each wrap with ⅓ cup of the veggie mixture and wrap them into a roll.
6. Bake for 15 minutes until golden brown and crispy, turning once.
7. Serve right away.

Variations & Ingredients Tips:

- Use different types of vegetables, such as carrots or sweet potatoes, for a variety of flavors and textures.
- Add some chopped nuts or raisins to the filling for extra flavor and crunch.
- Serve the samosa rolls with a side of chutney or yogurt sauce for dipping.

Per Serving: Calories: 230; Total Fat: 5g; Saturated Fat: 1g; Cholesterol: 0mg; Sodium: 160mg; Total Carbs: 41g; Fiber: 6g; Sugars: 5g; Protein: 7g

Orange Trail Oatmeal

Servings: 4 | Prep Time: 15 Minutes | Cooking Time: 20 Minutes

Ingredients:

- 1 1/2 cups quick-cooking oats
- 1/3 cup light brown sugar
- 1 egg
- 1 tsp orange zest
- 1 tbsp orange juice
- 2 tbsp whole milk
- 2 tbsp honey
- 2 tbsp butter, melted
- 2 tsp dried cranberries
- 1 tsp dried blueberries
- 1/8 tsp ground nutmeg
- Salt to taste
- 1/4 cup pecan pieces

Directions:

1. Preheat air fryer at 165°C/325°F.
2. Combine all ingredients in a bowl.
3. Press mixture into a greased cake pan.
4. Place pan in air fryer basket and roast for 8 minutes.
5. Let cool for 5 minutes before slicing and serving.

Variations & Ingredients Tips:

- Use old-fashioned oats for a heartier texture.
- Substitute maple syrup for the honey.
- Top with fresh berries and yogurt.

Per Serving: Calories: 305; Total Fat: 12g; Saturated Fat: 4g; Cholesterol: 50mg; Sodium: 75mg; Total Carbs: 45g; Dietary Fiber: 4g; Sugars: 23g; Protein: 6g

Shakshuka-style Pepper Cups

Servings: 4 | Prep Time: 15 Minutes | Cooking Time: 35 Minutes

Ingredients:

- 2 tbsp ricotta cheese crumbles
- 1 tbsp olive oil
- ½ yellow onion, diced
- 2 cloves garlic, minced
- ¼ tsp turmeric
- 1 can diced tomatoes
- 1 tbsp tomato paste
- ½ tsp smoked paprika
- ½ tsp salt
- ½ tsp granular sugar
- ¼ tsp ground cumin
- ¼ tsp ground coriander
- ⅛ tsp cayenne pepper
- 4 bell peppers
- 4 eggs
- 2 tbsp chopped basil

Directions:

1. Warm oil in a pan, stir-fry onion 10 mins until soft. Stir in garlic and turmeric 1 min.
2. Add tomatoes, paste, spices, salt and sugar. Remove from heat.
3. Preheat air fryer to 180°C/350°F. Slice pepper tops off and core.
4. Put peppers in basket, fill with tomato mix. Crack 1 egg into each pepper.
5. Bake 8-10 mins, top with ricotta, bake 1 min more.
6. Rest 5 mins, garnish with basil.

Variations & Ingredients Tips:

- Use different colored bell peppers for variety.
- Substitute goat cheese or feta for ricotta.

▶ Add cooked chorizo or ground meat to the sauce.

Per Serving: Calories: 155; Total Fat: 8g; Saturated Fat: 2g; Cholesterol: 195mg; Sodium: 505mg; Total Carbs: 14g; Dietary Fiber: 3g; Total Sugars: 8g; Protein: 9g

Chocolate Almond Crescent Rolls

Servings: 4 | Prep Time: 10 Minutes | Cooking Time: 8 Minutes

Ingredients:

- 1 (225 g) tube of crescent roll dough
- 170 g semi-sweet or bittersweet chocolate chunks
- 1 egg white, lightly beaten
- ¼ cup sliced almonds
- Powdered sugar, for dusting
- Butter or oil

Directions:

1. Preheat the air fryer to 180°C/350°F.
2. Unwrap the crescent roll dough and separate it into triangles with the points facing away from you. Place a row of chocolate chunks along the bottom edge of the dough. (If you are using chips, make it a double row.) Roll the dough up around the chocolate and then place another row of chunks on the dough. Roll again and finish with one or two chocolate chunks. Be sure to leave the end free of chocolate so that it can adhere to the rest of the roll.
3. Brush the tops of the crescent rolls with the lightly beaten egg white and sprinkle the almonds on top, pressing them into the crescent dough so they adhere.
4. Brush the bottom of the air fryer basket with butter or oil and transfer the crescent rolls to the basket. Air-fry at 180°C/350°F for 8 minutes.
5. Remove and let the crescent rolls cool before dusting with powdered sugar and serving.

Variations & Ingredients Tips:

▶ Use different types of chocolate, such as milk chocolate or white chocolate, for a variety of flavors.
▶ Add some cinnamon or nutmeg to the crescent dough for a spiced twist.
▶ Serve the crescent rolls with a side of fresh berries or whipped cream for a decadent breakfast or dessert.

Per Serving: Calories: 400; Total Fat: 24g; Saturated Fat: 10g; Cholesterol: 0mg; Sodium: 330mg; Total Carbs: 42g; Fiber: 3g; Sugars: 20g; Protein: 7g

Southwest Cornbread

Servings: 6 | Prep Time: 10 Minutes | Cooking Time: 18 Minutes

Ingredients:

- cooking spray
- ½ cup yellow cornmeal
- ½ cup flour
- 2 teaspoons baking powder
- ½ teaspoon salt
- ½ cup frozen corn kernels, thawed and drained
- ¼ cup finely chopped onion
- 1 or 2 small jalapeño peppers, seeded and chopped
- 1 egg
- ½ cup milk
- 2 tablespoons melted butter
- 55g sharp Cheddar cheese, grated

Directions:

1. Preheat air fryer to 180°C/360°F.
2. Spray baking pan with cooking spray.
3. Mix cornmeal, flour, baking powder and salt in a bowl.
4. Stir in corn, onion and jalapeños.
5. In another bowl, whisk egg, milk and butter. Add to dry ingredients.
6. Spoon half batter into pan, top with cheese, then remaining batter.
7. Cook for 18 mins until top is crispy and brown.

Variations & Ingredients Tips:

▶ Use canned or frozen corn instead of fresh.
▶ Add crumbled chorizo or cooked bacon to the batter.
▶ Top with sliced scallions or diced tomatoes before baking.

Per Serving: Calories: 217; Total Fat: 10g; Saturated Fat: 6g; Cholesterol: 54mg; Sodium: 445mg; Total Carbs: 26g; Dietary Fiber: 2g; Total Sugars: 2g; Protein: 7g

Soft Pretzels

Servings: 12 | Prep Time: 20 Minutes | Cooking Time: 6 Minutes

Ingredients:

- 2 teaspoons yeast
- 1 cup water, warm

- 1 teaspoon sugar
- 1 teaspoon salt
- 2½ cups all-purpose flour
- 2 tablespoons butter, melted
- 1 cup boiling water
- 1 tablespoon baking soda
- coarse sea salt
- melted butter

Directions:

1. Combine yeast and warm water in a small bowl.
2. In mixer bowl, mix sugar, salt and flour. With mixer running, add yeast mix and melted butter. Knead 10 mins.
3. Shape into a ball, let rise 1 hour.
4. Punch down dough and divide into 12-48 pieces depending on desired pretzel size.
5. Roll each into a rope and shape into pretzel/knot.
6. Combine boiling water and baking soda in a bowl. Let cool slightly.
7. Working in batches, dip pretzels in baking soda water for 30-60 secs then place on parchment. Sprinkle with salt.
8. Preheat air fryer to 175°C/350°F. Air fry in batches for 3 mins per side.
9. Brush pretzels with melted butter when done.

Variations & Ingredients Tips:

- Add cheese, herbs or spices to the dough before shaping.
- Substitute some of the all-purpose flour with whole wheat.
- Serve with mustard, cheese sauce or other dipping sauces.

Per Serving: Calories: 118; Total Fat: 2g; Saturated Fat: 1g; Cholesterol: 5mg; Sodium: 706mg; Total Carbs: 21g; Dietary Fiber: 1g; Total Sugars: 0g; Protein: 3g

Mediterranean Granola

Servings: 6 | Prep Time: 10 Minutes | Cooking Time: 40 Minutes

Ingredients:

- 1 cup rolled oats
- 1/4 cup dried cherries, diced
- 1/4 cup almond slivers
- 1/4 cup hazelnuts, chopped
- 1/4 cup pepitas
- 1/4 cup hemp hearts
- 3 tbsp honey
- 1 tbsp olive oil
- 1 tsp ground cinnamon
- 1/4 tsp ground nutmeg
- 1/4 tsp salt
- 2 tbsp dark chocolate chips
- 3 cups Greek yogurt

Directions:

1. Preheat air fryer to 130°C/260°F.
2. Stir the oats, cherries, almonds, hazelnuts, pepitas, hemp hearts, 2 tbsp of honey, olive oil, cinnamon, nutmeg, and salt in a bowl, mixing well.
3. Pour the mixture onto the parchment-lined frying basket and spread it into a single layer. Bake for 25-30 minutes, shaking twice.
4. Let the granola cool completely. Stir in the chocolate chips.
5. Divide between 6 cups. Top with Greek yogurt and remaining honey to serve.

Variations & Ingredients Tips:

- Use dried apricots, figs or dates instead of cherries.
- Add some chia seeds or flax meal for extra nutrition.
- Serve with milk, almond milk or coconut yogurt.

Per Serving: Calories: 370; Total Fat: 18g; Saturated Fat: 4g; Cholesterol: 5mg; Sodium: 105mg; Total Carbs: 43g; Dietary Fiber: 6g; Total Sugars: 21g; Protein: 15g

Baked Eggs

Servings: 4 | Prep Time: 5 Minutes | Cooking Time: 6 Minutes

Ingredients:

- 4 large eggs
- ⅛ teaspoon black pepper
- ⅛ teaspoon salt

Directions:

1. Preheat the air fryer to 165°C/330°F. Place 4 silicone muffin liners into the air fryer basket.
2. Crack 1 egg at a time into each silicone muffin liner. Sprinkle with black pepper and salt.
3. Bake for 6 minutes. Remove and let cool 2 minutes prior to serving.

Variations & Ingredients Tips:

- Add shredded cheese, chopped herbs or cooked meats on top of eggs before baking.
- Use ramekins or oven-safe bowls instead of silicone

liners.

Per Serving: Calories: 70; Total Fat: 5g; Saturated Fat: 1.5g; Cholesterol: 185mg; Sodium: 115mg; Total Carbs: 0g; Dietary Fiber: 0g; Total Sugars: 0g; Protein: 6g

Apple-cinnamon-walnut Muffins

Servings: 8 | Prep Time: 15 Minutes | Cooking Time: 11 Minutes

Ingredients:

- 1 cup flour
- ⅓ cup sugar
- 1 teaspoon baking powder
- ¼ teaspoon baking soda
- ¼ teaspoon salt
- 1 teaspoon cinnamon
- ¼ teaspoon ginger
- ¼ teaspoon nutmeg
- 1 egg
- 2 tablespoons pancake syrup, plus 2 teaspoons
- 2 tablespoons melted butter, plus 2 teaspoons
- ¾ cup unsweetened applesauce
- ½ teaspoon vanilla extract
- ¼ cup chopped walnuts
- ¼ cup diced apple
- 8 foil muffin cups, liners removed and sprayed with cooking spray

Directions:

1. Preheat air fryer to 165°C/330°F.
2. In a large bowl, stir together flour, sugar, baking powder, baking soda, salt, cinnamon, ginger, and nutmeg.
3. In a small bowl, beat egg until frothy. Add syrup, butter, applesauce, and vanilla and mix well.
4. Pour egg mixture into dry ingredients and stir just until moistened.
5. Gently stir in nuts and diced apple.
6. Divide batter among the 8 muffin cups.
7. Place 4 muffin cups in air fryer basket and cook at 165°C/330°F for 11 minutes.
8. Repeat with remaining 4 muffins or until toothpick inserted in center comes out clean.

Variations & Ingredients Tips:

- Substitute whole wheat flour for part of the all-purpose flour
- Add raisins or other dried fruit
- Use muffin liners instead of foil cups

Per Serving: Calories: 175; Total Fat: 7g; Saturated Fat: 2g; Cholesterol: 30mg; Sodium: 180mg; Total Carbs: 26g; Dietary Fiber: 2g; Total Sugars: 13g; Protein: 3g

Blueberry Applesauce Oat Cake

Servings: 4 | Prep Time: 10 Minutes | Cooking Time: 65 Minutes

Ingredients:

- 1 cup applesauce
- 2/3 cup quick-cooking oats
- ½ tsp baking powder
- A pinch of salt
- ½ cup almond milk
- 5 tbsp almond flour
- 1 tbsp honey
- 1 egg
- 1 tsp vanilla extract
- ½ cup blueberries
- 4 tbsp grape preserves

Directions:

1. In a bowl, combine oats, baking powder, and salt.
2. In a larger bowl, combine milk, almond flour, honey, egg, and vanilla with a whisk until well mixed.
3. Add applesauce and stir until combined, then add the oat mixture.
4. Gently fold in blueberries.
5. Pour mixture into a greased baking dish. Spoon preserves over the top, but do not stir in.
6. Preheat air fryer to 149°C/300°F.
7. Place baking dish in air fryer and bake 25 minutes until golden and set.
8. Remove and allow to cool 10-15 minutes before slicing into 4 pieces. Serve warm.

Variations & Ingredients Tips:

- Use frozen or fresh berries.
- Substitute maple syrup for the honey.
- Top with a crumble topping before baking.

Per Serving: Calories: 220; Total Fat: 5g; Saturated Fat: 0.5g; Cholesterol: 35mg; Sodium: 85mg; Total Carbs: 40g; Dietary Fiber: 4g; Total Sugars: 20g; Protein: 5g

Ham & Cheese Sandwiches

Servings: 2 | Prep Time: 5 Minutes | Cooking Time: 15 Minutes

Ingredients:

- 5 g butter
- 4 bread slices
- 4 deli ham slices
- 4 Cheddar cheese slices
- 4 thick tomato slices
- 1 teaspoon dried oregano

Directions:

1. Preheat air fryer to 190°C/370°F. Smear 2 g of butter on only one side of each slice of bread and sprinkle with oregano. On one of the slices, layer 2 slices of ham, 2 slices of cheese, and 2 slices of tomato on the unbuttered side. Place the unbuttered side of another piece of bread onto the toppings. Place the sandwiches butter side down into the air fryer. Bake for 8 minutes, flipping once until crispy. Let cool slightly, cut in half and serve.

Variations & Ingredients Tips:

- Use turkey, roast beef or salami instead of ham.
- Swap cheddar for Swiss, provolone or pepper Jack cheese.
- Add some sliced avocado, pickles or roasted red peppers for extra flavor.

Per Serving: Calories: 477; Total Fat: 28g; Saturated Fat: 15g; Cholesterol: 97mg; Sodium: 1477mg; Total Carbs: 29g; Dietary Fiber: 2g; Total Sugars: 6g; Protein: 29g

Vodka Basil Muffins With Strawberries

Servings: 6 | Prep Time: 10 Minutes | Cooking Time: 20 Minutes

Ingredients:

- ½ cup flour
- ½ cup granular sugar
- ½ tsp baking powder
- ⅛ tsp salt
- ½ cup chopped strawberries
- ¼ tsp vanilla extract
- 3 tbsp butter, melted
- 2 eggs
- ¼ tsp vodka
- 1 tbsp chopped basil

Directions:

1. Preheat air fryer to 190°C/375°F.
2. Combine the dry ingredients in a bowl. Set aside.
3. In another bowl, whisk the wet ingredients.
4. Pour wet ingredients into the bowl with the dry ingredients and gently combine.
5. Add basil and vodka to the batter. Do not overmix.
6. Spoon batter into six silicone cupcake liners lightly greased with olive oil.
7. Place liners in the frying basket and Bake for 7 minutes.
8. Let cool for 5 minutes onto a cooling rack before serving.

Variations & Ingredients Tips:

- Use other fresh herbs like thyme or rosemary instead of basil.
- Top with a lemon glaze or powdered sugar before serving.
- Add shredded zucchini or carrots to the batter for extra moisture.

Per Serving: Calories: 180; Total Fat: 8g; Saturated Fat: 4g; Cholesterol: 80mg; Sodium: 120mg; Total Carbs: 24g; Dietary Fiber: 1g; Total Sugars: 15g; Protein: 3g

Green Egg Quiche

Servings: 4 | Prep Time: 10 Minutes | Cooking Time: 30 Minutes

Ingredients:

- 1 cup broccoli florets
- 2 cups baby spinach
- 2 garlic cloves, minced
- ¼ teaspoon ground nutmeg
- 1 tablespoon olive oil
- Salt and pepper to taste
- 4 eggs
- 2 scallions, chopped
- 1 red onion, chopped
- 1 tablespoon sour cream
- 113 g grated fontina cheese

Directions:

1. Preheat air fryer to 190°C/375°F. Combine broccoli, spinach, onion, garlic, nutmeg, olive oil, and salt in a medium bowl, tossing to coat. Arrange the broccoli in a single layer in the parchment-lined frying basket and cook for 5 minutes. Remove and set to the side.

2. Use the same medium bowl to whisk eggs, salt, pepper, scallions, and sour cream. Add the roasted broccoli and 28 g fontina cheese until all ingredients are well combined. Pour the mixture into a greased baking dish and top with cheese. Bake in the air fryer for 15-18 minutes

until the center is set. Serve and enjoy.

Variations & Ingredients Tips:

- Use asparagus, zucchini or bell peppers instead of broccoli.
- Swap fontina for goat cheese, feta or Parmesan.
- Serve with a simple green salad and crusty bread for a light meal.

Per Serving: Calories: 264; Total Fat: 19g; Saturated Fat: 8g; Cholesterol: 227mg; Sodium: 336mg; Total Carbs: 8g; Dietary Fiber: 2g; Total Sugars: 3g; Protein: 16g

Appetizers And Snacks

Blooming Onion

Servings: 4 | Prep Time: 20 Minutes | Cooking Time: 25 Minutes

Ingredients:

- 1 large Vidalia onion, peeled
- 2 eggs
- 120 ml milk
- 1 cup flour
- 1 teaspoon salt
- ½ teaspoon freshly ground black pepper
- ¼ teaspoon ground cayenne pepper
- ½ teaspoon paprika
- ½ teaspoon garlic powder
- Dipping Sauce:
- ½ cup mayonnaise
- ½ cup ketchup
- 1 teaspoon Worcestershire sauce
- ½ teaspoon ground cayenne pepper
- ½ teaspoon paprika
- ½ teaspoon onion powder

Directions:

1. Cut off the top 2-cm of the onion, leaving the root end of the onion intact. Place the now flat, stem end of the onion down on a cutting board with the root end facing up. Make 16 slices around the onion, starting with your knife tip 1 cm away from the root so that you never slice through the root. Begin by making slices at 12, 3, 6 and 9 o'clock around the onion. Then make three slices down the onion in between each of the original four slices. Turn the onion over, gently separate the onion petals, and remove the loose pieces of onion in the center.
2. Combine the eggs and milk in a bowl. In a second bowl, combine the flour, salt, black pepper, cayenne pepper, paprika, and garlic powder.
3. Preheat the air fryer to 175°C/350°F.
4. Place the onion cut side up into a third empty bowl. Sprinkle the flour mixture all over the onion to cover it and get in between the onion petals. Turn the onion over to carefully shake off the excess flour and then transfer the onion to the empty flour bowl, again cut side up.
5. Pour the egg mixture all over the onion to cover all the flour. Let it soak for a minute in the mixture. Carefully remove the onion, tipping it upside down to drain off any excess egg, and transfer it to the empty egg bowl, again cut side up.
6. Finally, sprinkle the flour mixture over the onion a second time, making sure the onion is well coated and all the petals have the seasoned flour mixture on them. Carefully turn the onion over, shake off any excess flour and transfer it to a plate or baking sheet. Spray the onion generously with vegetable oil.
7. Transfer the onion, cut side up to the air fryer basket and air-fry for 25 minutes. The onion petals will open more fully as it cooks, so spray with more vegetable oil at least twice during the cooking time.
8. While the onion is cooking, make the dipping sauce by combining all the dip ingredients and mixing well. Serve the Blooming Onion as soon as it comes out of the air fryer with dipping sauce on the side.

Variations & Ingredients Tips:

- Use a yellow or white onion instead of Vidalia.
- Add some dried herbs like thyme or oregano to the flour mixture.

▶ Serve with ranch dressing or spicy aioli for dipping.

Per Serving: Calories: 430; Total Fat: 27g; Saturated Fat: 5g; Cholesterol: 98mg; Sodium: 1315mg; Total Carbs: 41g; Dietary Fiber: 3g; Total Sugars: 11g; Protein: 8g

Fiery Bacon-wrapped Dates

Servings: 16 | Prep Time: 15 Minutes | Cooking Time: 6 Minutes

Ingredients:

- 8 Thin-cut bacon strips, halved widthwise (gluten-free, if a concern)
- 16 Medium or large Medjool dates, pitted
- 3 tablespoons (about 20 g) Shredded semi-firm mozzarella
- 32 Pickled jalapeño rings

Directions:

1. Preheat the air fryer to 200°C/400°F.
2. Lay a bacon strip half on a clean, dry work surface. Split one date lengthwise without cutting through it, so that it opens like a pocket. Set it on one end of the bacon strip and open it a bit. Place 1 teaspoon of the shredded cheese and 2 pickled jalapeño rings in the date, then gently squeeze it together without fully closing it (just to hold the stuffing inside). Roll up the date in the bacon strip and set it bacon seam side down on a cutting board. Repeat this process with the remaining bacon strip halves, dates, cheese, and jalapeño rings.
3. Place the bacon-wrapped dates bacon seam side down in the basket. Air-fry undisturbed for 6 minutes, or until crisp and brown.
4. Use kitchen tongs to gently transfer the wrapped dates to a wire rack or serving platter. Cool for a few minutes before serving.

Variations & Ingredients Tips:

▶ Stuff the dates with blue cheese, goat cheese or cream cheese instead of mozzarella.
▶ Wrap the dates with prosciutto or pancetta instead of bacon.
▶ Drizzle with honey, balsamic glaze or hot honey before serving.

Per Serving: Calories: 57; Total Fat: 2g; Saturated Fat: 1g; Cholesterol: 6mg; Sodium: 117mg; Total Carbs: 9g; Dietary Fiber: 1g; Total Sugars: 8g; Protein: 2g

Garlic Wings

Servings: 4 | Prep Time: 10 Minutes | Cooking Time: 15 Minutes

Ingredients:

- 900 g chicken wings
- oil for misting
- cooking spray
- Marinade
- 1 cup buttermilk
- 2 cloves garlic, mashed flat
- 1 teaspoon Worcestershire sauce
- 1 bay leaf
- Coating
- 1½ cups grated Parmesan cheese
- ¾ cup breadcrumbs
- 1½ tablespoons garlic powder
- ½ teaspoon salt

Directions:

1. Mix all marinade ingredients together.
2. Remove wing tips (the third joint) and discard or freeze for stock. Cut the remaining wings at the joint and toss them into the marinade, stirring to coat well. Refrigerate for at least an hour but no more than 8 hours.
3. When ready to cook, combine all coating ingredients in a shallow dish.
4. Remove wings from marinade, shaking off excess, and roll in coating mixture. Press coating into wings so that it sticks well. Spray wings with oil.
5. Spray air fryer basket with cooking spray. Place wings in basket in single layer, close but not touching.
6. Cook at 180°C/360°F for 15 minutes or until chicken is done and juices run clear.
7. Repeat previous step to cook remaining wings.

Variations & Ingredients Tips:

▶ Use plain yogurt instead of buttermilk for the marinade.
▶ Add some smoked paprika, onion powder or dried herbs to the coating mixture.
▶ Serve with ranch dressing, blue cheese dip or honey mustard sauce.

Per Serving: Calories: 647; Total Fat: 37g; Saturated Fat: 15g; Cholesterol: 191mg; Sodium: 1227mg; Total Carbs: 21g; Dietary Fiber: 1g; Total Sugars: 4g; Protein: 55g

Chinese-style Potstickers

Servings: 6 | Prep Time: 20 Minutes | Cooking Time: 30 Minutes

Ingredients:

- 1 cup shredded Chinese cabbage
- ¼ cup chopped shiitake mushrooms
- ¼ cup grated carrots
- 2 tbsp minced chives
- 2 garlic cloves, minced
- 2 tsp grated fresh ginger
- 12 dumpling wrappers
- 2 tsp sesame oil

Directions:

1. Preheat air fryer to 190°C/370°F. Toss the Chinese cabbage, shiitake mushrooms, carrots, chives, garlic, and ginger in a baking pan and stir. Place the pan in the fryer and Bake for 3-6 minutes. Put a dumpling wrapper on a clean workspace, then top with a tablespoon of the veggie mix.
2. Fold the wrapper in half to form a half-circle and use water to seal the edges. Repeat with remaining wrappers and filling. Brush the potstickers with sesame oil and arrange them on the frying basket. Air Fry for 5 minutes until the bottoms should are golden brown. Take the pan out, add 1 tbsp of water, and put it back in the fryer to Air Fry for 4-6 minutes longer. Serve hot.

Variations & Ingredients Tips:

- Use ground pork, chicken or shrimp instead of vegetables for a meaty filling.
- Serve with soy sauce, rice vinegar and chili oil for dipping.
- Make a double batch and freeze extras for quick meals later.

Per Serving: Calories: 93; Total Fat: 2g; Saturated Fat: 0g; Cholesterol: 1mg; Sodium: 148mg; Total Carbs: 15g; Dietary Fiber: 1g; Total Sugars: 1g; Protein: 3g

Honey Tater Tots With Bacon

Servings: 4 | Prep Time: 5 Minutes | Cooking Time: 25 Minutes

Ingredients:

- 24 frozen tater tots
- 6 bacon slices
- 1 tbsp honey
- 1 cup grated cheddar

Directions:

1. Preheat air fryer to 200°C/400°F. Air Fry the tater tots for 10 minutes, shaking the basket once halfway through cooking. Cut the bacon into pieces. When the tater tots are done, remove them from the fryer to a baking pan. Top them with bacon and drizzle with honey. Air Fry for 5 minutes to crisp up the bacon. Top the tater tots with cheese and cook for 2 minutes to melt the cheese. Serve.

Variations & Ingredients Tips:

- Use sweet potato tater tots for a healthier twist.
- Add some chopped green onions or jalapeños for extra flavor.
- Drizzle with ranch dressing or BBQ sauce before serving.

Per Serving: Calories: 342; Total Fat: 21g; Saturated Fat: 9g; Cholesterol: 47mg; Sodium: 691mg; Total Carbs: 26g; Dietary Fiber: 1g; Total Sugars: 6g; Protein: 14g

Caponata Salsa

Servings: 6 | Prep Time: 10 Minutes | Cooking Time: 16 Minutes

Ingredients:

- 4 cups (450 g eggplant) Purple Italian eggplant(s), stemmed and diced (no need to peel)
- Olive oil spray
- 1½ cups Celery, thinly sliced
- 16 (about 225 g) Cherry or grape tomatoes, halved
- 1 tablespoon Drained and rinsed capers, chopped
- Up to 1 tablespoon Minced fresh rosemary leaves
- 1½ tablespoons Red wine vinegar
- 1½ teaspoons Granulated white sugar
- ¾ teaspoon Table salt
- ¾ teaspoon Ground black pepper

Directions:

1. Preheat the air fryer to 175°C/350°F.
2. Put the eggplant pieces in a bowl and generously coat them with olive oil spray. Toss and stir, spray again, and toss some more, until the pieces are glistening.
3. When the machine is at temperature, pour the eggplant pieces into the basket and spread them out into an even layer. Air-fry for 8 minutes, tossing and rearrang-

ing the pieces twice.
4. Meanwhile, put the celery and tomatoes in the same bowl the eggplant pieces had been in. Generously coat them with olive oil spray; then toss well, spray again, and toss some more, until the vegetables are well coated.
5. When the eggplant has cooked for 8 minutes, pour the celery and tomatoes on top in the basket. Air-fry undisturbed for 8 minutes more, until the tomatoes have begun to soften.
6. Pour the contents of the basket back into the same bowl. Add the capers, rosemary, vinegar, sugar, salt, and pepper. Toss well to blend, breaking up the tomatoes a bit to create more moisture in the mixture.
7. Cover and refrigerate for 2 hours to blend the flavors. Serve chilled or at room temperature. The caponata salsa can stay in its covered bowl in the fridge for up to 2 days before the vegetables weep too much moisture and the dish becomes too wet.

Variations & Ingredients Tips:

- Add some chopped olives, pine nuts or raisins for extra flavor and texture.
- Drizzle with balsamic glaze before serving.
- Serve as a topping for crostini, bruschetta or grilled meats.

Per Serving: Calories: 103; Total Fat: 3g; Saturated Fat: 0g; Cholesterol: 0mg; Sodium: 419mg; Total Carbs: 19g; Dietary Fiber: 6g; Total Sugars: 11g; Protein: 3g

Apple Rollups

Servings: 8 | Prep Time: 10 Minutes | Cooking Time: 5 Minutes

Ingredients:

- 8 slices whole wheat sandwich bread
- 113 g Colby Jack cheese, grated
- ½ small apple, chopped
- 2 tablespoons butter, melted

Directions:

1. Remove crusts from bread and flatten the slices with rolling pin. Don't be gentle. Press hard so that bread will be very thin.
2. Top bread slices with cheese and chopped apple, dividing the ingredients evenly.
3. Roll up each slice tightly and secure each with one or two toothpicks.
4. Brush outside of rolls with melted butter.
5. Place in air fryer basket and cook at 200°C/390°F for 5 minutes, until outside is crisp and nicely browned.

Variations & Ingredients Tips:

- Try different cheeses like cheddar, brie or goat cheese.
- Substitute pears or peaches for the apples.
- Sprinkle with cinnamon-sugar before cooking for a sweet twist.

Per Serving: Calories: 169; Cholesterol: 19 mg; Total Fat: 10g; Saturated Fat: 6g: Sodium: 245mg; Total Carbohydrates: 16 g; Dietary Fiber: 2g; Total Sugars: 4 g; Protein: 7 g

Cheesy Spinach Dip(2)

Servings: 8 | Prep Time: 15 Minutes | Cooking Time: 30 Minutes

Ingredients:

- 1 can refrigerated biscuit dough
- 115 g cream cheese, softened
- ¼ cup mayonnaise
- 1 cup spinach
- 60 g cooked bacon, crumbled
- 2 scallions, chopped
- 2 cups grated Fontina cheese
- 1 cup grated cheddar
- ½ tsp garlic powder

Directions:

1. Preheat the air fryer to 175°C/350°F. Divide the dough into 8 biscuits and press each one into and up the sides of the silicone muffin cup, then set aside. Combine the cream cheese and mayonnaise and beat until smooth. Stir in the spinach, bacon, scallions, 1 cup of cheddar cheese and garlic powder. Then divide the mixture between the muffin cups. Put them in the basket and top each with 1 tbsp of Fontina cheese. Bake for 8-13 minutes or until the dough is golden and the filling is hot and bubbling. Remove from the air fryer and cool on a wire rack. Serve.

Variations & Ingredients Tips:

- Add some diced jalapeños or hot sauce for a spicy kick.
- Use Swiss, Gruyère or Gouda cheese instead of Fontina.
- Garnish with chopped tomatoes, red onions or fresh herbs.

Per Serving: Calories: 355; Total Fat: 25g; Saturated Fat: 13g; Cholesterol: 61mg; Sodium: 657mg; Total Carbs: 19g; Dietary Fiber: 1g; Total Sugars: 3g; Protein: 15g

Avocado Fries With Quick Salsa Fresca

Servings: 4 | Prep Time: 20 Minutes| Cooking Time: 6 Minutes

Ingredients:

- ½ cup flour
- 2 teaspoons salt
- 2 eggs, lightly beaten
- 1 cup panko breadcrumbs*
- ⅛ teaspoon cayenne pepper
- ¼ teaspoon smoked paprika (optional)
- 2 large avocados, just ripe
- vegetable oil, in a spray bottle
- Quick Salsa Fresca
- 1 cup cherry tomatoes
- 1 2.5 cm chunk of shallot or red onion
- 2 teaspoons fresh lime juice
- 1 teaspoon chopped fresh cilantro or parsley
- salt and freshly ground black pepper

Directions:

1. Set up a dredging station with three shallow dishes. Place the flour and salt in the first shallow dish. Place the eggs into the second dish. Combine the breadcrumbs, cayenne pepper and paprika (if using) in the third dish.
2. Preheat the air fryer to 200°C/400°F.
3. Cut the avocado in half around the pit and separate the two sides. Slice the avocados into long strips while still in their skin. Run a spoon around the slices, separating them from the avocado skin. Try to keep the slices whole, but don't worry if they break – you can still coat and air-fry the pieces.
4. Coat the avocado slices by dredging them first in the flour, then the egg and then the breadcrumbs, pressing the crumbs on gently with your hands. Set the coated avocado fries on a tray and spray them on all sides with vegetable oil.
5. Air-fry the avocado fries, one layer at a time, at 200°C/400°F for 6 minutes, turning them over halfway through the cooking time and spraying lightly again if necessary. When the fries are nicely browned on all sides, season with salt and remove.
6. While the avocado fries are air-frying, make the salsa fresca by combining everything in a food processor. Pulse several times until the salsa is a chunky purée. Serve the fries warm with the salsa on the side for dipping.

Variations & Ingredients Tips:

▸ Use plantains instead of avocados for a Caribbean twist.
▸ Add some grated Parmesan to the breadcrumb mixture.
▸ Serve with a creamy cilantro-lime dipping sauce.

Per Serving: Calories: 401; Total Fat: 27g; Saturated Fat: 5g; Cholesterol: 93mg; Sodium: 1188mg; Total Carbs: 35g; Dietary Fiber: 9g; Total Sugars: 4g; Protein: 9g

Beef Steak Sliders

Servings: 8 | Prep Time: 10 Minutes | Cooking Time: 22 Minutes

Ingredients:

- 450 g top sirloin steaks, about 2 cm thick
- salt and pepper
- 2 large onions, thinly sliced
- 1 tablespoon extra-light olive oil
- 8 slider buns
- Horseradish Mayonnaise
- 1 cup light mayonnaise
- 4 teaspoons prepared horseradish
- 2 teaspoons Worcestershire sauce
- 1 teaspoon coarse brown mustard

Directions:

1. Place steak in air fryer basket and cook at 200°C/390°F for 6 minutes. Turn and cook 6 more minutes for medium rare. If you prefer your steak medium, continue cooking for 3 minutes.
2. While the steak is cooking, prepare the Horseradish Mayonnaise by mixing all ingredients together.
3. When steak is cooked, remove from air fryer, sprinkle with salt and pepper to taste, and set aside to rest.
4. Toss the onion slices with the oil and place in air fryer basket. Cook at 200°C/390°F for 7 minutes, until onion rings are soft and browned.
5. Slice steak into very thin slices.
6. Spread slider buns with the horseradish mayo and pile on the meat and onions. Serve with remaining horseradish dressing for dipping.

Variations & Ingredients Tips:

▸ Use Hawaiian rolls or mini pretzel buns instead of slider buns.
▸ Top with crumbled blue cheese or crispy fried onions.
▸ Serve with roasted garlic aioli or chimichurri sauce.

Per Serving: Calories: 406; Total Fat: 26g; Saturated Fat: 5g; Cholesterol: 57mg; Sodium: 515mg; Total Carbs: 23g; Dietary Fiber: 2g; Total Sugars: 5g; Protein: 22g

Garlic Breadsticks

Servings: 12 | Prep Time: 10 Minutes | Cooking Time: 7 Minutes

Ingredients:

- 1½ tablespoons Olive oil
- 1½ teaspoons Minced garlic
- ¼ teaspoon Table salt
- ¼ teaspoon Ground black pepper
- 170 g Purchased pizza dough (vegan dough, if that's a concern)

Directions:

1. Preheat the air fryer to 200°C/400°F. Mix the oil, garlic, salt, and pepper in a small bowl.
2. Divide the pizza dough into 4 balls for a small air fryer, 6 for a medium machine, or 8 for a large, each ball about the size of a walnut in its shell. (Each should weigh 30 g, if you want to drag out a scale and get obsessive.) Roll each ball into a 13 cm long stick under your clean palms on a clean, dry work surface. Brush the sticks with the oil mixture.
3. When the machine is at temperature, place the prepared dough sticks in the basket, leaving a 2.5 cm space between them. Air-fry undisturbed for 7 minutes, or until puffed, golden, and set to the touch.
4. Use kitchen tongs to gently transfer the breadsticks to a wire rack and repeat step 3 with the remaining dough sticks.

Variations & Ingredients Tips:

- Sprinkle the breadsticks with grated Parmesan, sesame seeds or everything bagel seasoning before cooking.
- Serve with marinara sauce, garlic butter or ranch dressing for dipping.
- Make a sweet version by brushing with cinnamon-sugar butter instead of garlic oil.

Per Serving: Calories: 58; Total Fat: 3g; Saturated Fat: 0g; Cholesterol: 0mg; Sodium: 105mg; Total Carbs: 7g; Dietary Fiber: 0g; Total Sugars: 0g; Protein: 1g

Balsamic Grape Dip

Servings: 6 | Prep Time: 5 Minutes | Cooking Time: 25 Minutes

Ingredients:

- 2 cups seedless red grapes
- 1 tbsp balsamic vinegar
- 1 tbsp honey
- 1 cup Greek yogurt
- 2 tbsp milk
- 2 tbsp minced fresh basil

Directions:

1. Preheat air fryer to 190°C/380°F. Add the grapes and balsamic vinegar to the frying basket, then pour honey over and toss to coat. Roast for 8-12 minutes, shriveling the grapes, and take them out of the air fryer. Mix the milk and yogurt together, then gently stir in the grapes and basil. Serve and enjoy!

Variations & Ingredients Tips:

- Use different types of grapes like green or black for variety.
- Substitute the honey with maple syrup or agave nectar.
- Add some chopped nuts like pistachios or almonds for crunch.

Per Serving: Calories: 89; Total Fat: 1g; Saturated Fat: 1g; Cholesterol: 2mg; Sodium: 20mg; Total Carbs: 16g; Dietary Fiber: 1g; Total Sugars: 14g; Protein: 4g

Arancini With Sun-dried Tomatoes And Mozzarella

Servings: 6 | Prep Time: 20 Minutes | Cooking Time: 15 Minutes

Ingredients:

- 1 tablespoon olive oil
- ½ small onion, finely chopped
- 1 cup Arborio rice
- ¼ cup white wine or dry vermouth
- 1 cup vegetable or chicken stock
- 1½ cups water
- 1 teaspoon salt
- freshly ground black pepper
- ⅓ cup grated Parmigiano-Reggiano cheese
- 56-85 g mozzarella cheese
- 2 eggs, lightly beaten
- ¼ cup chopped oil-packed sun-dried tomatoes
- 1½ cups Italian seasoned breadcrumbs, divided
- olive oil
- marinara sauce, for serving

Directions:

1. Start by cooking the Arborio rice.
2. Stovetop Method: Preheat a medium saucepan over medium heat. Add the olive oil and sauté the onion until it starts to become tender – about 5 minutes. Add the rice and stir well to coat all the grains of rice. Add the white wine or vermouth. Let this simmer and get absorbed by the rice. Then add the stock and water, cover, reduce the heat to low and simmer for 20 minutes.
3. Pressure-Cooker Method: Preheat the pressure cooker using the BROWN setting. Add the oil and cook the onion for a few minutes. Add the rice, wine, stock, water, salt and freshly ground black pepper, give everything one good stir and lock the lid in place. Pressure cook on HIGH for 7 minutes. Reduce the pressure with the QUICK-RELEASE method and carefully remove the lid.
4. Taste the rice to make sure it is tender. Season with salt and freshly ground black pepper and stir in the grated Parmigiano-Reggiano cheese. Spread the rice out onto a baking sheet to cool.
5. While the rice is cooling, cut the mozzarella into 2 cm cubes.
6. Once the rice has cooled, combine the rice with the eggs, sun-dried tomatoes and ½ cup of the breadcrumbs. Place the remaining breadcrumbs in a shallow dish. Shape the rice mixture into 12 balls. Press a hole in the rice ball with your finger and push one or two cubes of mozzarella cheese into the hole. Mold the rice back into a ball, enclosing the cheese. Roll the finished rice balls in the breadcrumbs and place them on a baking sheet while you make the remaining rice balls. Spray or brush the rice balls with olive oil.
7. Preheat the air fryer to 190°C/380°F.
8. Cook 6 arancini at a time. Air-fry for 10 minutes. Gently turn the arancini over, brush or spray with oil again and air-fry for another 5 minutes. Serve warm with the marinara sauce.

Variations & Ingredients Tips:

- Add some chopped prosciutto or pancetta for a meaty flavor.
- Use fontina, provolone or smoked mozzarella instead of regular mozzarella.
- Serve with a lemon-garlic aioli for dipping.

Per Serving: Calories: 405; Cholesterol: 81mg; Total Fat: 18g; Saturated Fat: 5g; Sodium: 1015mg; Total Carbohydrates: 45 g; Dietary Fiber: 3g; Total Sugars: 4g; Protein 16 g

Spicy Chicken And Pepper Jack Cheese Bites

Servings: 8 | Prep Time: 20 Minutes + Chilling Time | Cooking Time: 8 Minutes

Ingredients:

- 225 g cream cheese, softened
- 2 cups grated pepper jack cheese
- 1 jalapeño pepper, diced
- 2 scallions, minced
- 1 tsp paprika
- 2 tsp salt, divided
- 3 cups shredded cooked chicken
- ¼ cup all-purpose flour*
- 2 eggs, lightly beaten
- 1 cup panko breadcrumbs*
- olive oil, in a spray bottle
- salsa

Directions:

1. Beat the cream cheese in a bowl until it is smooth and easy to stir. Add the pepper jack cheese, jalapeño pepper, scallions, paprika and 1 teaspoon of salt. Fold in the shredded cooked chicken and combine well. Roll this mixture into 2.5-cm balls. Set up a dredging station with three shallow dishes. Place the flour into one shallow dish. Place the eggs into a second shallow dish. Finally, combine the panko breadcrumbs and remaining teaspoon of salt in a third dish. Coat the chicken cheese balls by rolling each ball in the flour first, then dip them into the eggs and finally roll them in the panko breadcrumbs to coat all sides. Refrigerate for at least 30 minutes. Preheat the air fryer to 200°C/400°F. Spray the chicken cheese balls with oil and air-fry in batches for 8 minutes. Shake the basket a few times throughout the cooking process to help the balls brown evenly. Serve hot with salsa on the side.

Variations & Ingredients Tips:

- Use a mixture of cheddar, mozzarella, and Parmesan cheese for a milder flavor.
- Add chopped bacon, ham, or chorizo for a meatier bite.
- Serve with ranch dressing, honey mustard, or BBQ sauce for dipping.

Per Serving: Calories: 341; Total Fat: 24g; Saturated Fat: 12g; Cholesterol: 143mg; Sodium: 892mg; Total Carbohydrates: 9g; Dietary Fiber: 1g; Total Sugars: 1g; Protein: 23g

Basil Feta Crostini

Servings: 4 | Prep Time: 5 Minutes | Cooking Time: 10 Minutes

Ingredients:

- 1 baguette, sliced
- ¼ cup olive oil
- 2 garlic cloves, minced
- 113 g feta cheese
- 2 tbsp basil, minced

Directions:

1. Preheat air fryer to 190°C/380°F. Combine together the olive oil and garlic in a bowl. Brush it over one side of each slice of bread. Put the bread in a single layer in the frying basket and Bake for 5 minutes. In a small bowl, mix together the feta cheese and basil. Remove the toast from the air fryer, then spread a thin layer of the feta cheese mixture over the top of each piece. Serve.

Variations & Ingredients Tips:

- Use goat cheese or ricotta instead of feta for a milder flavor.
- Top with diced tomatoes or roasted red peppers for added color and taste.
- Drizzle with balsamic glaze or honey before serving.

Per Serving: Calories: 364; Total Fat: 19g; Saturated Fat: 7g; Cholesterol: 33mg; Sodium: 674mg; Total Carbs: 38g; Dietary Fiber: 1g; Total Sugars: 1g; Protein: 11g

Crunchy Parmesan Edamame

Servings: 4 | Prep Time: 5 Minutes | Cooking Time: 25 Minutes + Cooling Time

Ingredients:

- 1 cup edamame, shelled
- 1 tbsp sesame oil
- 1 tsp five-spice powder
- ½ tsp salt
- ½ tsp garlic powder
- ¼ cup grated Parmesan

Directions:

1. Cook the edamame in boiling salted water until crisp-tender, about 10 minutes. Drain and leave to cool. Preheat air fryer to 175°C/350°F. Combine edamame, garlic, and sesame oil in a bowl. Place them in the frying basket and Air Fry for 16 minutes, shaking twice. Transfer to a small bowl and toss with five-spice powder and salt. Serve chilled topped with Parmesan cheese. Enjoy!

Variations & Ingredients Tips:

- Use frozen shelled edamame for convenience.

- Substitute soy sauce or tamari for the salt.
- Sprinkle with toasted sesame seeds or furikake seasoning.

Per Serving: Calories: 127; Total Fat: 8g; Saturated Fat: 2g; Cholesterol: 4mg; Sodium: 405mg; Total Carbs: 8g; Dietary Fiber: 3g; Total Sugars: 2g; Protein: 7g

Barbecue Chicken Nachos

Servings: 3 | Prep Time: 10 Minutes | Cooking Time: 5 Minutes

Ingredients:

- 3 heaping cups (a little more than 85 g) Corn tortilla chips (gluten-free, if a concern)
- ¾ cup Shredded deboned and skinned rotisserie chicken meat (gluten-free, if a concern)
- 3 tablespoons Canned black beans, drained and rinsed
- 9 rings Pickled jalapeño slices
- 4 Small pickled cocktail onions, halved
- 3 tablespoons Barbecue sauce (any sort)
- ¾ cup (about 85 g) Shredded Cheddar cheese

Directions:

1. Preheat the air fryer to 200°C/400°F.
2. Cut a circle of parchment paper to line a 15 cm round cake pan for a small air fryer, an 18 cm round cake pan for a medium air fryer, or a 20 cm round cake pan for a large machine.
3. Fill the pan with an even layer of about two-thirds of the chips. Sprinkle the chicken evenly over the chips. Set the pan in the basket and air-fry undisturbed for 2 minutes.
4. Remove the basket from the machine. Scatter the beans, jalapeño rings, and pickled onion halves over the chicken. Drizzle the barbecue sauce over everything, then sprinkle the cheese on top.
5. Return the basket to the machine and air-fry undisturbed for 3 minutes, or until the cheese has melted and is bubbly. Remove the pan from the machine and cool for a couple of minutes before serving.

Variations & Ingredients Tips:

- Use pork carnitas or ground beef instead of chicken.
- Add sliced avocado or guacamole on top after cooking.
- Serve with sour cream, salsa and chopped cilantro.

Per Serving: Calories: 386; Total Fat: 20g; Saturated Fat: 9g; Cholesterol: 59mg; Sodium: 808mg; Total Carbs: 31g; Dietary Fiber: 5g; Total Sugars: 8g; Protein: 22g

Cheese Straws

Servings: 8 | Prep Time: 15 Minutes | Cooking Time: 7 Minutes

Ingredients:

- For dusting All-purpose flour
- Two quarters of one thawed sheet (that is, a half of the sheet cut into two even pieces; wrap and refreeze the remainder) A 490 g box frozen puff pastry
- 1 Large egg(s)
- 2 tablespoons Water
- ¼ cup (about 20 g) Finely grated Parmesan cheese
- up to 1 teaspoon Ground black pepper

Directions:

1. Preheat the air fryer to 200°C/400°F.
2. Dust a clean, dry work surface with flour. Set one of the pieces of puff pastry on top, dust the pastry lightly with flour, and roll with a rolling pin to a 15 cm square.
3. Whisk the egg(s) and water in a small or medium bowl until uniform. Brush the pastry square(s) generously with this mixture. Sprinkle each square with 2 tablespoons grated cheese and up to ½ teaspoon ground black pepper.
4. Cut each square into 4 even strips. Grasp each end of 1 strip with clean, dry hands; twist it into a cheese straw. Place the twisted straws on a baking sheet.
5. Lay as many straws as will fit in the air-fryer basket—as a general rule, 4 of them in a small machine, 5 in a medium model, or 6 in a large. There should be space for air to circulate around the straws. Set the baking sheet with any remaining straws in the fridge.
6. Air-fry undisturbed for 7 minutes, or until puffed and crisp. Use tongs to transfer the cheese straws to a wire rack, then make subsequent batches in the same way (keeping the baking sheet with the remaining straws in the fridge as each batch cooks). Serve warm.

Variations & Ingredients Tips:

▸ Add some smoked paprika, garlic powder or cayenne pepper to the cheese mixture.
▸ Brush with pesto or sun-dried tomato paste before sprinkling with cheese.
▸ Serve alongside soup, salad or as a party appetizer.

Per Serving: Calories: 157; Total Fat: 11g; Saturated Fat: 3g; Cholesterol: 27mg; Sodium: 117mg; Total Carbs: 11g; Dietary Fiber: 0g; Total Sugars: 0g; Protein: 4g

Beer Battered Onion Rings

Servings: 2 | Prep Time: 20 Minutes | Cooking Time: 16 Minutes

Ingredients:

- 80 g flour
- ½ teaspoon baking soda
- 1 teaspoon paprika
- 1 teaspoon salt
- ½ teaspoon freshly ground black pepper
- 180 ml beer
- 1 egg, beaten
- 1½ cups fine breadcrumbs
- 1 large Vidalia onion, peeled and sliced into 13 mm rings
- vegetable oil

Directions:

1. Set up a dredging station. Mix the flour, baking soda, paprika, salt and pepper together in a bowl. Pour in the beer, add the egg and whisk until smooth. Place the breadcrumbs in a cake pan or shallow dish.
2. Separate the onion slices into individual rings. Dip each onion ring into the batter with a fork. Lift the onion ring out of the batter and let any excess batter drip off. Then place the onion ring in the breadcrumbs and shake the cake pan back and forth to coat the battered onion ring. Pat the ring gently with your hands to make sure the breadcrumbs stick and that both sides of the ring are covered. Place the coated onion ring on a sheet pan and repeat with the rest of the onion rings.
3. Preheat the air fryer to 180°C/360°F.
4. Lightly spray the onion rings with oil, coating both sides. Layer the onion rings in the air fryer basket, stacking them on top of each other in a haphazard manner.
5. Air-fry for 10 minutes at 180°C/360°F. Flip the onion rings over and rotate the onion rings from the bottom of the basket to the top. Air-fry for an additional 6 minutes.
6. Serve immediately with your favorite dipping sauce.

Variations & Ingredients Tips:

▸ Use sparkling water instead of beer for a non-alcoholic version.
▸ Add some cayenne pepper or hot sauce to the batter for a spicy kick.
▸ Serve with ranch dressing, chipotle mayo or marinara sauce for dipping.

Per Serving: Calories: 456; Total Fat: 12g; Saturated Fat: 2g; Cholesterol: 93mg; Sodium: 1733mg; Total Carbs: 71g; Dietary Fiber: 5g; Total Sugars: 8g; Protein: 14g

Greek Street Tacos

Servings: 8 | Prep Time: 10 Minutes | Cooking Time: 3 Minutes

Ingredients:

- 8 small flour tortillas (10 cm diameter)
- 8 tablespoons hummus
- 4 tablespoons crumbled feta cheese
- 4 tablespoons chopped kalamata or other olives (optional)
- olive oil for misting

Directions:

1. Place 1 tablespoon of hummus or tapenade in the center of each tortilla. Top with 1 teaspoon of feta crumbles and 1 teaspoon of chopped olives, if using.
2. Using your finger or a small spoon, moisten the edges of the tortilla all around with water.
3. Fold tortilla over to make a half-moon shape. Press center gently. Then press the edges firmly to seal in the filling.
4. Mist both sides with olive oil.
5. Place in air fryer basket very close but try not to overlap.
6. Cook at 200°C/390°F for 3 minutes, just until lightly browned and crispy.

Variations & Ingredients Tips:

- Use pita bread, naan or flatbread instead of tortillas.
- Add some diced tomatoes, cucumbers or red onions to the filling.
- Drizzle with tzatziki sauce, balsamic glaze or hot sauce before serving.

Per Serving: Calories: 125; Total Fat: 5g; Saturated Fat: 1g; Cholesterol: 6mg; Sodium: 263mg; Total Carbs: 17g; Dietary Fiber: 1g; Total Sugars: 0g; Protein: 4g

Poultry Recipes

Tortilla Crusted Chicken Breast

Servings: 2 | Prep Time: 10 Minutes | Cooking Time: 12 Minutes

Ingredients:

- 1/3 cup flour
- 1 teaspoon salt
- 1 1/2 teaspoons chili powder
- 1 teaspoon ground cumin
- Freshly ground black pepper
- 1 egg, beaten
- 3/4 cup coarsely crushed yellow corn tortilla chips
- 2 (85-115g) boneless chicken breasts
- Vegetable oil
- 1/2 cup salsa
- 1/2 cup crumbled queso fresco
- Fresh cilantro leaves
- Sour cream or guacamole (optional)

Directions:

1. Set up 3 dishes: one with flour+salt+chili powder+cumin+pepper, one with beaten egg, one with crushed tortilla chips.
2. Dredge chicken in flour, then egg, then tortilla chips, pressing to adhere.
3. Spray chicken with oil on both sides.
4. Preheat air fryer to 195°C/380°F.
5. Air fry chicken for 6 mins, flip and cook 6 more mins.
6. Serve with salsa, queso fresco, cilantro, and sour cream/guacamole if desired.

Variations & Ingredients Tips:

- Use panko breadcrumbs instead of tortilla chips.
- Add lime zest or jalapeño to the breading.
- Serve with Mexican rice and beans on the side.

Per Serving: Calories: 471; Total Fat: 19g; Saturated Fat: 4g; Cholesterol: 200mg; Sodium: 1205mg; Total Carbs:

37g; Dietary Fiber: 3g; Total Sugars: 2g; Protein: 36g

Spinach And Feta Stuffed Chicken Breasts

Servings: 4 | Prep Time: 15 Minutes | Cooking Time: 27 Minutes

Ingredients:

- 1 (285g) package frozen spinach, thawed and drained well
- 1 cup feta cheese, crumbled
- 1/2 teaspoon freshly ground black pepper
- 4 boneless chicken breasts
- Salt and freshly ground black pepper
- 1 tablespoon olive oil

Directions: | **Prepare the filling. Squeeze out as much liquid as possible from the thawed spinach. Rough chop the spinach and transfer it to a mixing bowl with the feta cheese and the freshly ground black pepper.** | **Prepare the chicken breast. Place the chicken breast on a cutting board and press down on the chicken breast with one hand to keep it stabilized. Make an incision about 2.5cm long in the fattest side of the breast. Move the knife up and down inside the chicken breast, without poking through either the top or the bottom, or the other side of the breast. The inside pocket should be about 7.5cm long, but the opening should only be about 2.5cm wide. If this is too difficult, you can make the incision longer, but you will have to be more careful when cooking the chicken breast since this will expose more of the stuffing.**

7. Once you have prepared the chicken breasts, use your fingers to stuff the filling into each pocket, spreading the mixture down as far as you can.
8. Preheat the air fryer to 195°C/380°F.
9. Lightly brush or spray the air fryer basket and the chicken breasts with olive oil. Transfer two of the stuffed chicken breasts to the air fryer. Air-fry for 12 minutes, turning the chicken breasts over halfway through the cooking time. Remove the chicken to a resting plate and air-fry the second two breasts for 12 minutes. Return the first batch of chicken to the air fryer with the second batch and air-fry for 3 more minutes. When the chicken is cooked, an instant read thermometer should register 75°C/165°F in the thickest part of the chicken, as well as in the stuffing.
10. Remove the chicken breasts and let them rest on a cutting board for 2 to 3 minutes. Slice the chicken on the bias and serve with the slices fanned out.

Variations & Ingredients Tips:

- Use fresh spinach instead of frozen.
- Substitute feta for goat cheese or shredded mozzarella.
- Add sun-dried tomatoes or pine nuts to the stuffing mixture.

Per Serving: Calories: 332; Total Fat: 14g; Saturated Fat: 7g; Cholesterol: 143mg; Sodium: 599mg; Total Carbs: 6g; Dietary Fiber: 2g; Total Sugars: 2g; Protein: 44g

Buttermilk-fried Drumsticks

Servings: 2 | Prep Time: 15 Minutes | Cooking Time: 25 Minutes

Ingredients:

- 1 egg
- ½ cup buttermilk
- ¾ cup self-rising flour
- ¾ cup seasoned panko breadcrumbs
- 1 teaspoon salt
- ¼ teaspoon ground black pepper (to mix into coating)
- 4 chicken drumsticks, skin on
- oil for misting or cooking spray

Directions:

1. Beat together egg and buttermilk in shallow dish.
2. In a second shallow dish, combine the flour, panko crumbs, salt, and pepper.
3. Sprinkle chicken legs with additional salt and pepper to taste.
4. Dip legs in buttermilk mixture, then roll in panko mixture, pressing in crumbs to make coating stick. Mist with oil or cooking spray.
5. Spray air fryer basket with cooking spray.
6. Cook drumsticks at 180°C/360°F for 10 minutes. Turn pieces over and cook an additional 10 minutes.
7. Turn pieces to check for browning. If you have any white spots that haven't begun to brown, spritz them with oil or cooking spray. Continue cooking for 5 more minutes or until crust is golden brown and juices run clear. Larger, meatier drumsticks will take longer to cook than small ones.

Variations & Ingredients Tips:

- Use drumettes or chicken wings instead of drumsticks for smaller portions.
- Add dried herbs like thyme, rosemary, or oregano to the flour mixture for extra flavor.
- Serve with honey mustard, ranch, or BBQ sauce for dipping.

Per Serving: Calories: 610; Total Fat: 28g; Saturated Fat: 7g; Sodium: 1580mg; Total Carbohydrates: 47g; Dietary Fiber: 2g; Total Sugars: 4g; Protein: 43g

Restaurant-style Chicken Thighs

Servings: 4 | Prep Time: 5 Minutes (plus 10 Minutes Marinating Time) | Cooking Time: 30 Minutes

Ingredients:

- 454 grams boneless, skinless chicken thighs
- ¼ cup barbecue sauce
- 2 cloves garlic, minced
- 1 tsp lemon zest
- 2 tbsp parsley, chopped
- 2 tbsp lemon juice

Directions:

1. Coat the chicken with barbecue sauce, garlic, and lemon juice in a medium bowl. leave to marinate for 10 minutes.
2. Preheat air fryer to 190°C/380°F.
3. When ready to cook, remove the chicken from the bowl and shake off any drips. Arrange the chicken in the air fryer and Bake for 16-18 minutes, until golden and cooked through.
4. Serve topped with lemon zest and parsley. Enjoy!

Variations & Ingredients Tips:

- Use honey mustard, teriyaki, or pesto sauce instead of BBQ for different flavors.
- Add sliced onions, peppers, or mushrooms to the marinade for extra veggies.
- Serve with sweet potato fries, coleslaw, or grilled corn on the side.

Per Serving: Calories: 250; Total Fat: 11g; Saturated Fat: 2.5g; Sodium: 440mg; Total Carbohydrates: 8g; Dietary Fiber: 0g; Total Sugars: 6g; Protein: 29g

Honey Lemon Thyme Glazed Cornish Hen

Servings: 2 | Prep Time: 10 Minutes | Cooking Time: 20 Minutes

Ingredients:

- 1 (900g) Cornish game hen, split in half
- Olive oil
- Salt and freshly ground black pepper
- 1/4 teaspoon dried thyme
- 1/4 cup honey
- 1 tablespoon lemon zest
- Juice of 1 lemon
- 1 1/2 teaspoons chopped fresh thyme leaves
- 1/2 teaspoon soy sauce
- Freshly ground black pepper

Directions:

1. Split the game hen in half by cutting down each side of the backbone and then cutting through the breast. Brush or spray both halves of the game hen with the olive oil and then season with the salt, pepper and dried thyme.
2. Preheat the air fryer to 200°C/390°F.
3. Place the game hen, skin side down, into the air fryer and air-fry for 5 minutes. Turn the hen halves over and air-fry for 10 minutes.
4. While the hen is cooking, combine the honey, lemon zest and juice, fresh thyme, soy sauce and pepper in a small bowl.
5. When the air fryer timer rings, brush the honey glaze onto the game hen and continue to air-fry for another 3 to 5 minutes, just until the hen is nicely glazed, browned and has an internal temperature of 74°C/165°F.
6. Let the hen rest for 5 minutes and serve warm.

Variations & Ingredients Tips:

- Use orange instead of lemon for a different citrus flavor.
- Add some minced garlic or ginger to the glaze.
- Stuff the cavity with lemon wedges and thyme sprigs before cooking.

Per Serving: Calories: 520; Total Fat: 28g; Saturated Fat: 7g; Cholesterol: 240mg; Sodium: 490mg; Total Carbs: 29g; Dietary Fiber: 0g; Total Sugars: 27g; Protein: 45g

Chicken Strips

Servings: 4 | Prep Time: 10 Minutes (plus 30 Minutes Marinating Time) | Cooking Time: 8 Minutes

Ingredients:

- 454 grams chicken tenders
- Marinade
- ¼ cup olive oil
- 2 tablespoons water
- 2 tablespoons honey

- 2 tablespoons white vinegar
- ½ teaspoon salt
- ½ teaspoon crushed red pepper
- 1 teaspoon garlic powder
- 1 teaspoon onion powder
- ½ teaspoon paprika

Directions:

1. Combine all marinade ingredients and mix well.
2. Add chicken and stir to coat. Cover tightly and let marinate in refrigerator for 30 minutes.
3. Remove tenders from marinade and place them in a single layer in the air fryer basket.
4. Cook at 200°C/390°F for 3 minutes. Turn tenders over and cook for 5 minutes longer or until chicken is done and juices run clear.
5. Repeat step 4 to cook remaining tenders.

Variations & Ingredients Tips:

- Use boneless, skinless chicken breasts cut into strips instead of tenders.
- Add a dash of Worcestershire sauce or soy sauce to the marinade for extra umami flavor.
- Serve with ranch dressing, honey mustard, or BBQ sauce for dipping.

Per Serving: Calories: 290; Total Fat: 15g; Saturated Fat: 2.5g; Sodium: 370mg; Total Carbohydrates: 9g; Dietary Fiber: 0g; Total Sugars: 8g; Protein: 30g

Prosciutto Chicken Rolls

Servings: 4 | Prep Time: 20 Minutes | Cooking Time: 30 Minutes

Ingredients:

- 1/2 cup chopped broccoli
- 1/2 cup grated cheddar
- 2 scallions, sliced
- 2 garlic cloves, minced
- 4 prosciutto thin slices
- 1/4 cup cream cheese
- Salt and pepper to taste
- 1/2 tsp dried oregano
- 1/2 tsp dried basil
- 4 chicken breasts
- 2 tbsp chopped cilantro

Directions:

1. Preheat air fryer to 190°C/375°F.
2. Combine broccoli, scallion, garlic, Cheddar, cream cheese, salt, pepper, oregano, and basil in a small bowl. | Prepare the chicken by placing it between two pieces of plastic wrap. Pound the chicken with a meat mallet or heavy can until it is evenly 1.25 cm thickness.
3. Top each with a slice of prosciutto and spoon 1/4 of the cheese mixture in the center of the chicken breast. Fold each breast over the filling and transfer to a greased baking dish.
4. Place the dish in the frying basket and bake for 8 minutes. Flip the chicken and bake for another 8-12 minutes.
5. Allow resting for 5 minutes. Serve warm sprinkled with cilantro and enjoy!

Variations & Ingredients Tips:

- Use spinach, sundried tomatoes or roasted red peppers in the filling.
- Wrap the chicken with bacon instead of prosciutto.
- Drizzle with a balsamic glaze before serving.

Per Serving: Calories: 340; Total Fat: 17g; Saturated Fat: 9g; Cholesterol: 145mg; Sodium: 610mg; Total Carbs: 3g; Dietary Fiber: 1g; Total Sugars: 1g; Protein: 42g

Pickle Brined Fried Chicken

Servings: 4 | Prep Time: 20 Minutes (plus Brining Time) | Cooking Time: 47 Minutes

Ingredients:

- 4 bone-in, skin-on chicken legs, cut into drumsticks and thighs (about 1.6kg)
- Pickle juice from a 680g jar of kosher dill pickles
- 1/2 cup flour
- Salt and freshly ground black pepper
- 2 eggs
- 1 cup fine breadcrumbs
- 1 teaspoon salt
- 1 teaspoon freshly ground black pepper
- 1/2 teaspoon ground paprika
- 1/8 teaspoon ground cayenne pepper
- Vegetable or canola oil in a spray bottle

Directions:

1. Place the chicken in a shallow dish and pour the pickle juice over the top. Cover and transfer the chicken to the refrigerator to brine in the pickle juice for 3 to 8 hours.
2. When you are ready to cook, remove the chicken from the refrigerator to let it come to room temperature while you set up a dredging station. Place the flour in a shallow dish and season well with salt and freshly ground black pepper. Whisk the eggs in a second shal-

low dish. In a third shallow dish, combine the breadcrumbs, salt, pepper, paprika and cayenne pepper.
3. Preheat the air fryer to 190°C/370°F.
4. Remove the chicken from the pickle brine and gently dry it with a clean kitchen towel. Dredge each piece of chicken in the flour, then dip it into the egg mixture, and finally press it into the breadcrumb mixture to coat all sides of the chicken. Place the breaded chicken on a plate or baking sheet and spray each piece all over with vegetable oil.
5. Air-fry the chicken in two batches. Place two chicken thighs and two drumsticks into the air fryer basket. Air-fry for 10 minutes. Then, gently turn the chicken pieces over and air-fry for another 10 minutes. Remove the chicken pieces and let them rest on plate – do not cover. Repeat with the second batch of chicken, air-frying for 20 minutes, turning the chicken over halfway through.
6. Lower the temperature of the air fryer to 170°C/340°F. Place the first batch of chicken on top of the second batch already in the basket and air-fry for an additional 7 minutes.
7. Serve warm and enjoy.

Variations & Ingredients Tips:

- Use buttermilk instead of pickle juice for a traditional fried chicken brine.
- Add dried herbs like thyme, oregano or rosemary to the breading mix.
- Serve with hot sauce, honey or ranch dressing for dipping.

Per Serving: Calories: 620; Total Fat: 33g; Saturated Fat: 9g; Cholesterol: 295mg; Sodium: 2020mg; Total Carbs: 23g; Dietary Fiber: 1g; Total Sugars: 2g; Protein: 58g

Kale & Rice Chicken Rolls

Servings: 4 | Prep Time: 15 Minutes | Cooking Time: 35 Minutes

Ingredients:

- 4 boneless, skinless chicken thighs
- 1/2 tsp ground fenugreek seeds
- 1 cup cooked wild rice
- 2 sundried tomatoes, diced
- 1/2 cup chopped kale
- 2 garlic cloves, minced
- 1 tsp salt
- 1 lemon, juiced
- 1/2 cup crumbled feta
- 1 tbsp olive oil

Directions:

1. Preheat air fryer to 190°C/380°F.
2. Put the chicken thighs between two pieces of plastic wrap, and using a meat mallet or a rolling pin, pound them out to about 6-mm thick.
3. Combine the rice, tomatoes, kale, garlic, salt, fenugreek seeds and lemon juice in a bowl and mix well.
4. Divide the rice mixture among the chicken thighs and sprinkle with feta. Fold the sides of the chicken thigh over the filling, and then gently place each of them seam-side down into the greased air frying basket. Drizzle the stuffed chicken thighs with olive oil.
5. Roast the stuffed chicken thighs for 12 minutes, then turn them over and cook for an additional 10 minutes.
6. Serve and enjoy!

Variations & Ingredients Tips:

- Use spinach or chard instead of kale.
- Add some chopped nuts like pistachios or pine nuts to the filling.
- Drizzle with tzatziki sauce before serving.

Per Serving: Calories: 370; Total Fat: 21g; Saturated Fat: 7g; Cholesterol: 145mg; Sodium: 900mg; Total Carbs: 17g; Dietary Fiber: 2g; Total Sugars: 2g; Protein: 32g

Indian Chicken Tandoori

Servings: 2 | Prep Time: 10 Minutes (plus Marinating Time) | Cooking Time: 35 Minutes

Ingredients:

- 2 chicken breasts, cubed
- 1/2 cup hung curd
- 1 tsp turmeric powder
- 1 tsp red chili powder
- 1 tsp chaat masala powder
- Pinch of salt

Directions:

1. Preheat air fryer to 175°C/350°F.
2. Mix the hung curd, turmeric, red chili powder, chaat masala powder, and salt in a mixing bowl. Stir until the mixture is free of lumps.
3. Coat the chicken with the mixture, cover, and refrigerate for 30 minutes to marinate.
4. Place the marinated chicken chunks in a baking pan and drizzle with the remaining marinade.
5. Bake for 25 minutes until the chicken is juicy and spiced.
6. Serve warm.

Variations & Ingredients Tips:

- Use Greek yogurt instead of hung curd for a tangy flavor.
- Add minced garlic and ginger to the marinade for extra zing.
- Garnish with fresh cilantro and squeeze of lime juice.

Per Serving: Calories: 220; Total Fat: 3g; Saturated Fat: 1g; Cholesterol: 105mg; Sodium: 370mg; Total Carbs: 4g; Dietary Fiber: 1g; Total Sugars: 2g; Protein: 41g

Ranch Chicken Tortillas

Servings: 4 | Prep Time: 20 Minutes | Cooking Time: 35 Minutes

Ingredients:

- 2 chicken breasts
- 1 tbsp Ranch seasoning
- 1 tbsp taco seasoning
- 1 cup flour
- 1 egg
- ½ cup bread crumbs
- 4 flour tortillas
- 1 ½ cups shredded lettuce
- 3 tbsp ranch dressing
- 2 tbsp cilantro, chopped

Directions:

1. Preheat air fryer to 190°C/370°F.
2. Slice the chicken breasts into cutlets by cutting in half horizontally on a cutting board. Rub with ranch and taco seasonings.
3. In one shallow bowl, add flour. In another shallow bowl, beat the egg. In the third shallow bowl, add bread crumbs.
4. Lightly spray the air fryer basket with cooking oil. First, dip the cutlet in the flour, dredge in egg, and then finish by coating with bread crumbs.
5. Place the cutlets in the fryer and Bake for 6-8 minutes. Flip them and cook further for 4 minutes until crisp.
6. Allow the chicken to cook for a few minutes, then cut into strips. Divide into 4 equal portions along with shredded lettuce, ranch dressing, cilantro and tortillas.
7. Serve and enjoy!

Variations & Ingredients Tips:

- Use corn tortillas or lettuce wraps for a gluten-free option.
- Add sliced avocado, tomatoes, or jalapeños for extra toppings.
- Substitute ranch with blue cheese, Caesar, or chipotle dressing.

Per Serving: Calories: 450; Total Fat: 18g; Saturated Fat: 4g; Sodium: 920mg; Total Carbohydrates: 44g; Dietary Fiber: 3g; Total Sugars: 3g; Protein: 30g

Buttery Chicken Legs

Servings: 4 | Prep Time: 10 Minutes | Cooking Time: 50 Minutes

Ingredients:

- 1 tsp baking powder
- 1 tsp dried mustard
- 1 tsp smoked paprika
- 1 tsp garlic powder
- 1 tsp dried thyme
- Salt and pepper to taste
- 680 grams chicken legs
- 3 tbsp butter, melted

Directions:

1. Preheat air fryer to 190°C/370°F.
2. Combine all ingredients, except for butter, in a bowl until coated.
3. Place the chicken legs in the greased air fryer basket.
4. Air Fry for 18 minutes, flipping once and brushing with melted butter on both sides.
5. Let chill onto a serving plate for 5 minutes before serving.

Variations & Ingredients Tips:

- Use skinless chicken legs for a lower fat option.
- Add a pinch of cayenne pepper or red pepper flakes for a spicy kick.
- Serve with a side of coleslaw, potato salad, or roasted vegetables.

Per Serving: Calories: 400; Total Fat: 28g; Saturated Fat: 11g; Sodium: 260mg; Total Carbohydrates: 2g; Dietary Fiber: 1g; Total Sugars: 0g; Protein: 34g

Chicken Chunks

Servings: 4 | Prep Time: 10 Minutes | Cooking Time: 10 Minutes

Ingredients:

- 450g chicken tenders cut into 4cm chunks
- Salt and pepper
- 1/2 cup cornstarch
- 2 eggs, beaten

- 1 cup panko breadcrumbs
- Oil for misting or cooking spray

Directions:

1. Season chicken chunks with salt and pepper.
2. Dip chicken in cornstarch, then egg, then panko crumbs to coat well.
3. Spray chicken chunks with oil on all sides.
4. Place in a single layer in air fryer basket. Cook at 200°C/390°F for 5 minutes.
5. Spray with more oil, flip chunks and cook 5 more minutes until golden and cooked through.
6. Repeat steps 4-5 for remaining chicken chunks.

Variations & Ingredients Tips:

- Use chicken breast or thigh meat instead of tenders.
- Add spices like paprika or cajun seasoning to the breadcrumb coating.
- Serve with ranch, honey mustard or bbq sauce for dipping.

Per Serving: Calories: 384; Total Fat: 8g; Saturated Fat: 2g; Cholesterol: 150mg; Sodium: 264mg; Total Carbs: 42g; Dietary Fiber: 2g; Total Sugars: 1g; Protein: 34g

Coconut Chicken With Apricot-ginger Sauce

Servings: 4 | Prep Time: 20 Minutes | Cooking Time: 8 Minutes Per Batch

Ingredients:

- 680 grams boneless, skinless chicken tenders, cut in large chunks (about 3 cm)
- salt and pepper
- ½ cup cornstarch
- 2 eggs
- 1 tablespoon milk
- 3 cups shredded coconut (see below)
- oil for misting or cooking spray
- Apricot-Ginger Sauce
- ½ cup apricot preserves
- 2 tablespoons white vinegar
- ¼ teaspoon ground ginger
- ¼ teaspoon low-sodium soy sauce
- 2 teaspoons white or yellow onion, grated or finely minced

Directions:

1. Mix all ingredients for the Apricot-Ginger Sauce well and let sit for flavors to blend while you cook the chicken.
2. Season chicken chunks with salt and pepper to taste.
3. Place cornstarch in a shallow dish.
4. In another shallow dish, beat together eggs and milk.
5. Place coconut in a third shallow dish. (If also using panko breadcrumbs, as suggested below, stir them to mix well.)
6. Spray air fryer basket with oil or cooking spray.
7. Dip each chicken chunk into cornstarch, shake off excess, and dip in egg mixture.
8. Shake off excess egg mixture and roll lightly in coconut or coconut mixture. Spray with oil.
9. Place coated chicken chunks in air fryer basket in a single layer, close together but without sides touching.
10. Cook at 180°C/360°F for 4 minutes, stop, and turn chunks over.
11. Cook an additional 4 minutes or until chicken is done inside and coating is crispy brown.
12. Repeat steps 9 through 11 to cook remaining chicken chunks.

Variations & Ingredients Tips:

- Substitute apricot preserves with peach, mango, or pineapple for different fruity sauces.
- Add a pinch of cayenne pepper or red pepper flakes to the sauce for a spicy kick.
- Mix shredded coconut with panko breadcrumbs for an extra crispy coating.

Per Serving: Calories: 610; Total Fat: 29g; Saturated Fat: 20g; Sodium: 430mg; Total Carbohydrates: 52g; Dietary Fiber: 5g; Total Sugars: 29g; Protein: 39g

Southwest Gluten-free Turkey Meatloaf

Servings: 8 | Prep Time: 15 Minutes | Cooking Time: 35 Minutes

Ingredients:

- 454 grams lean ground turkey
- ¼ cup corn grits
- ¼ cup diced onion
- 1 teaspoon minced garlic
- ½ teaspoon black pepper
- ½ teaspoon salt
- 1 large egg
- ½ cup ketchup
- 4 teaspoons chipotle hot sauce
- ⅓ cup shredded cheddar cheese

Directions:

1. Preheat the air fryer to 180°C/350°F.

2. In a large bowl, mix together the ground turkey, corn grits, onion, garlic, black pepper, and salt.
3. In a small bowl, whisk the egg. Add the egg to the turkey mixture and combine.
4. In a small bowl, mix the ketchup and hot sauce. Set aside.
5. Liberally spray a 23x10-cm loaf pan with olive oil spray. Depending on the size of your air fryer, you may need to use 2 or 3 mini loaf pans.
6. Spoon the ground turkey mixture into the loaf pan and evenly top with half of the ketchup mixture. Cover with foil and place the meatloaf into the air fryer. Cook for 30 minutes; remove the foil and discard. Check the internal temperature (it should be nearing 74°C/165°F).
7. Coat the top of the meatloaf with the remaining ketchup mixture, and sprinkle the cheese over the top. Place the meatloaf back in the air fryer for the remaining 5 minutes (or until the internal temperature reaches 74°C/165°F).
8. Remove from the oven and let cool 5 minutes before serving. Serve warm with desired sides.

Variations & Ingredients Tips:

- Use ground chicken or pork instead of turkey for a different flavor.
- Add diced bell peppers, jalapeños, or corn kernels to the meatloaf mixture for extra veggies.
- Serve with a side of salsa, guacamole, or sour cream for dipping.

Per Serving: Calories: 170; Total Fat: 8g; Saturated Fat: 2.5g; Sodium: 420mg; Total Carbohydrates: 8g; Dietary Fiber: 1g; Total Sugars: 4g; Protein: 17g

Chicken Adobo

Servings: 6 | Prep Time: 10 Minutes (plus 1 Hour Marinating Time) | Cooking Time: 12 Minutes

Ingredients:

- 6 boneless chicken thighs
- ¼ cup soy sauce or tamari
- ½ cup rice wine vinegar
- 4 cloves garlic, minced
- ⅛ teaspoon crushed red pepper flakes
- ½ teaspoon black pepper

Directions:

1. Place the chicken thighs into a resealable plastic bag with the soy sauce or tamari, the rice wine vinegar, the garlic, and the crushed red pepper flakes. Seal the bag and let the chicken marinate at least 1 hour in the refrigerator.
2. Preheat the air fryer to 200°C/400°F.
3. Drain the chicken and pat dry with a paper towel. Season the chicken with black pepper and liberally spray with cooking spray.
4. Place the chicken in the air fryer basket and cook for 9 minutes, turn over at 9 minutes and check for an internal temperature of 74°C/165°F, and cook another 3 minutes.

Variations & Ingredients Tips:

- Use bone-in, skin-on chicken thighs for a juicier and crispier result.
- Add sliced onions or bell peppers to the marinade for extra flavor and texture.
- Serve with steamed rice, quinoa, or stir-fried vegetables for a complete meal.

Per Serving: Calories: 210; Total Fat: 9g; Saturated Fat: 2.5g; Sodium: 770mg; Total Carbohydrates: 2g; Dietary Fiber: 0g; Total Sugars: 0g; Protein: 27g

Crispy Duck With Cherry Sauce

Servings: 2 | Prep Time: 20 Minutes | Cooking Time: 33 Minutes

Ingredients:

- 1 whole duck (up to 2.3 kg), split in half, back and rib bones removed
- 1 teaspoon olive oil
- salt and freshly ground black pepper
- Cherry Sauce:
- 1 tablespoon butter
- 1 shallot, minced
- ½ cup sherry
- ¾ cup cherry preserves
- 1 cup chicken stock
- 1 teaspoon white wine vinegar
- 1 teaspoon fresh thyme leaves
- salt and freshly ground black pepper

Directions:

1. Preheat the air fryer to 200°C/400°F.
2. Trim some of the fat from the duck. Rub olive oil on the duck and season with salt and pepper. Place the duck halves in the air fryer basket, breast side up and facing the center of the basket.
3. Air-fry the duck for 20 minutes. Turn the duck over and air-fry for another 6 minutes.
4. While duck is air-frying, make the cherry sauce. Melt the butter in a large sauté pan. Add the shallot and sauté until it is just starting to brown – about 2 to 3 minutes. Add the sherry and deglaze the pan by scraping up any brown bits from the bottom of the pan. Simmer

the liquid for a few minutes, until it has reduced by half. Add the cherry preserves, chicken stock and white wine vinegar. Whisk well to combine all the ingredients. Simmer the sauce until it thickens and coats the back of a spoon – about 5 to 7 minutes. Season with salt and pepper and stir in the fresh thyme leaves.
5. When the air fryer timer goes off, spoon some cherry sauce over the duck and continue to air-fry at 200°C/400°F for 4 more minutes. Then, turn the duck halves back over so that the breast side is facing up. Spoon more cherry sauce over the top of the duck, covering the skin completely. Air-fry for 3 more minutes and then remove the duck to a plate to rest for a few minutes.
6. Serve the duck in halves, or cut each piece in half again for a smaller serving. Spoon any additional sauce over the duck or serve it on the side.

Variations & Ingredients Tips:

- Use duck breasts or legs instead of a whole duck for quicker cooking time.
- Substitute cherry preserves with blackberry, raspberry, or apricot jam.
- Garnish with fresh herbs like rosemary, sage, or parsley before serving.

Per Serving: Calories: 610; Total Fat: 36g; Saturated Fat: 12g; Sodium: 430mg; Total Carbohydrates: 41g; Dietary Fiber: 1g; Total Sugars: 34g; Protein: 34g

Cajun Chicken Livers

Servings: 2 | Prep Time: 30 Minutes (plus 2 Hours Marinating Time) | Cooking Time: 45 Minutes

Ingredients:

- 454 grams chicken livers, rinsed, connective tissue discarded
- 1 cup whole milk
- ½ cup cornmeal
- 3/4 cup flour
- 1 tsp salt and black pepper
- 1 tsp Cajun seasoning
- 2 eggs
- 1 ½ cups bread crumbs
- 1 tbsp olive oil
- 2 tbsp chopped parsley

Directions:

1. Pat chicken livers dry with paper towels, then transfer them to a small bowl and pour in the milk and black pepper. Let sit covered in the fridge for 2 hours.
2. Preheat air fryer at 190°C/375°F.
3. In a bowl, combine cornmeal, flour, salt, and Cajun seasoning. In another bowl, beat the eggs, and in a third bowl, add bread crumbs.
4. Dip chicken livers first in the cornmeal mixture, then in the egg, and finally in the bread crumbs.
5. Place chicken livers in the greased air fryer basket, brush the tops lightly with olive oil, and Air Fry for 16 minutes, turning once.
6. Serve right away sprinkled with parsley.

Variations & Ingredients Tips:

- Add a dash of hot sauce or cayenne pepper to the milk for extra spice.
- Serve with a side of remoulade sauce, hot sauce, or ranch dressing for dipping.
- Use a mixture of half cornmeal and half flour for a lighter coating.

Per Serving: Calories: 790; Total Fat: 30g; Saturated Fat: 9g; Sodium: 1530mg; Total Carbohydrates: 73g; Dietary Fiber: 4g; Total Sugars: 9g; Protein: 61g

Christmas Chicken & Roasted Grape Salad

Servings: 4 | Prep Time: 20 Minutes | Cooking Time: 40 Minutes

Ingredients:

- 3 chicken breasts, pat-dried
- 1 tsp paprika
- Salt and pepper to taste
- 2 cups seedless red grapes
- ½ cup mayonnaise
- ½ cup plain yogurt
- 2 tbsp honey mustard
- 2 tbsp fresh lemon juice
- 1 cup chopped celery
- 2 scallions, chopped
- 2 tbsp walnuts, chopped

Directions:

1. Preheat the air fryer to 190°C/370°F.
2. Sprinkle the chicken breasts with paprika, salt, and pepper. Transfer to the greased air fryer basket and Air Fry for 16-19 minutes, flipping once. Remove and set on a cutting board.
3. Put the grapes in the fryer and spray with cooking oil. Fry for 4 minutes or until the grapes are hot and tender.
4. Mix the mayonnaise, yogurt, honey mustard, and lem-

on juice in a bowl and whisk.

5. Cube the chicken and add to the dressing along with the grapes, walnuts, celery, and scallions. Toss gently and serve.

Variations & Ingredients Tips:

- Use turkey, duck, or Cornish game hen instead of chicken for a festive twist.
- Substitute grapes with dried cranberries, cherries, or figs.
- Add chopped apples, pears, or persimmons for a fruity crunch.

Per Serving: Calories: 450; Total Fat: 29g; Saturated Fat: 5g; Sodium: 400mg; Total Carbohydrates: 20g; Dietary Fiber: 2g; Total Sugars: 15g; Protein: 32g

Crunchy Chicken Strips

Servings: 4 | Prep Time: 15 Minutes | Cooking Time: 40 Minutes

Ingredients:

- 1 chicken breast, sliced into strips
- 1 tbsp grated Parmesan cheese
- 1 cup breadcrumbs
- 1 tbsp chicken seasoning
- 2 eggs, beaten
- Salt and pepper to taste

Directions:

1. Preheat air fryer to 180°C/350°F.
2. Mix the breadcrumbs, Parmesan cheese, chicken seasoning, salt, and pepper in a mixing bowl.
3. Coat the chicken with the crumb mixture, then dip in the beaten eggs. Finally, coat again with the dry ingredients.
4. Arrange the coated chicken pieces on the greased air fryer basket and Air Fry for 15 minutes. Turn over halfway through cooking and cook for another 15 minutes.
5. Serve immediately.

Variations & Ingredients Tips:

- Use panko breadcrumbs or crushed cornflakes for a crispier coating.
- Add garlic powder, onion powder, or paprika to the seasoning mix for extra flavor.
- Serve with honey mustard, ranch dressing, or ketchup for dipping.

Per Serving: Calories: 270; Total Fat: 8g; Saturated Fat: 2.5g; Sodium: 460mg; Total Carbohydrates: 22g; Dietary Fiber: 1g; Total Sugars: 2g; Protein: 25g

Beef, Pork & Lamb Recipes

Cheeseburger Sliders With Pickle Sauce

Servings: 4 | Prep Time: 15 Minutes | Cooking Time: 20 Minutes

Ingredients:

- 4 iceberg lettuce leaves, each halved lengthwise
- 2 red onion slices, rings separated
- 1/4 cup shredded Swiss cheese
- 450-g ground beef
- 1 tbsp Dijon mustard
- Salt and pepper to taste
- 1/4 tsp shallot powder
- 2 tbsp mayonnaise
- 2 tsp ketchup
- 1/2 tsp mustard powder
- 1/2 tsp dill pickle juice
- 1/8 tsp onion powder
- 1/8 tsp garlic powder
- 1/8 tsp sweet paprika
- 8 tomato slices
- 1/2 cucumber, thinly sliced

Directions:

1. In a large bowl, use your hands to mix beef, Swiss cheese, mustard, salt, shallot, and black pepper. Do not overmix. Form 8 patties 3-cm thick. Mix together mayonnaise, ketchup, mustard powder, pickle juice, onion and garlic powder, and paprika in a medium bowl. Stir until smooth.
2. Preheat air fryer to 200°C/400°F. Place the sliders in the greased frying basket and Air Fry for about 8-10 minutes, flipping once until preferred doneness. Serve on top of lettuce halves with a slice of tomato, a slider, onion, a smear of special sauce, and cucumber.

Variations & Ingredients Tips:

- Use ground turkey or chicken instead of beef for a leaner option
- Add bacon bits or crumbled bacon to the beef mixture
- Brush the buns with garlic butter or herb butter before toasting

Per Serving: Calories: 370; Total Fat: 26g; Saturated Fat: 8g; Cholesterol: 100mg; Sodium: 420mg; Total Carbohydrates: 6g; Dietary Fiber: 2g; Total Sugars: 4g; Protein: 29g

California Burritos

Servings: 4 | Prep Time: 15 Minutes | Cooking Time: 17 Minutes

Ingredients:

- 454g sirloin steak, sliced thin
- 1 teaspoon dried oregano
- 1 teaspoon ground cumin
- 1/2 teaspoon garlic powder
- 16 tater tots
- 1/3 cup sour cream
- 1/2 lime, juiced
- 2 tablespoons hot sauce
- 1 large avocado, pitted
- 1 teaspoon salt, divided
- 4 large (20-25cm) flour tortillas
- 1/2 cup shredded cheddar cheese or Monterey jack
- 2 tablespoons avocado oil

Directions:

1. Preheat the air fryer to 380°F/193°C.
2. Season the steak with oregano, cumin, and garlic powder. Place the steak on one side of the air fryer and the tater tots on the other side. (It's okay for them to touch, because the flavors will all come together in the burrito.) Cook for 8 minutes, toss, and cook an additional 4 to 6 minutes.
3. Meanwhile, in a small bowl, stir together the sour cream, lime juice, and hot sauce.
4. In another small bowl, mash together the avocado and season with 1/2 teaspoon of the salt, to taste.
5. To assemble the burrito, lay out the tortillas, equally divide the meat amongst the tortillas. Season the steak equally with the remaining 1/2 teaspoon salt. Then layer the mashed avocado and sour cream mixture on top. Top each tortilla with 4 tater tots and finish each with 2 tablespoons cheese. Roll up the sides and, while holding in the sides, roll up the burrito. Place the burritos in the air fryer basket and brush with avocado oil (working in batches as needed); cook for 3 minutes or until lightly golden on the outside.

Variations & Ingredients Tips:

- Use flour or whole wheat tortillas instead of plain for more flavor and nutrients
- Add sautéed peppers and onions to the filling for extra veggies
- Substitute black beans or refried beans for the tater tots

Per Serving: Calories: 852; Total Fat: 42g; Saturated Fat: 16g; Cholesterol: 147mg; Sodium: 1168mg; Total Carbs: 72g; Dietary Fiber: 9g; Total Sugars: 4g; Protein: 48g

Pork Taco Gorditas

Servings: 4 | Prep Time: 20 Minutes | Cooking Time: 21 Minutes

Ingredients:

- 454 g lean ground pork
- 2 tablespoons chili powder
- 2 tablespoons ground cumin
- 1 teaspoon dried oregano
- 2 teaspoons paprika
- 1 teaspoon garlic powder
- ½ cup water
- 1 (425-g) can pinto beans, drained and rinsed
- ½ cup taco sauce
- salt and freshly ground black pepper
- 2 cups grated Cheddar cheese
- 5 (30-cm) flour tortillas
- 4 (20 cm) crispy corn tortilla shells
- 4 cups shredded lettuce
- 1 tomato, diced
- ⅓ cup sliced black olives

- sour cream, for serving
- tomato salsa, for serving

Directions:

1. Preheat the air fryer to 200°C/400°F.
2. Place the ground pork in the air fryer basket and air-fry at 200°C/400°F for 10 minutes, stirring a few times during the cooking process to gently break up the meat. Combine the chili powder, cumin, oregano, paprika, garlic powder and water in a small bowl. Stir the spice mixture into the browned pork. Stir in the beans and taco sauce and air-fry for an additional minute. Transfer the pork mixture to a bowl. Season to taste with salt and freshly ground black pepper.
3. Sprinkle ½ cup of the shredded cheese in the center of four of the flour tortillas, making sure to leave a 5 cm border around the edge free of cheese and filling. Divide the pork mixture among the four tortillas, placing it on top of the cheese. Place a crunchy corn tortilla on top of the pork and top with shredded lettuce, diced tomatoes, and black olives. Cut the remaining flour tortilla into 4 quarters. These quarters of tortilla will serve as the bottom of the gordita. Place one quarter tortilla on top of each gordita and fold the edges of the bottom flour tortilla up over the sides, enclosing the filling. While holding the seams down, brush the bottom of the gordita with olive oil and place the seam side down on the countertop while you finish the remaining three gorditas.
4. Preheat the air fryer to 190°C/380°F.
5. Air-fry one gordita at a time. Transfer the gordita carefully to the air fryer basket, seam side down. Brush or spray the top tortilla with oil and air-fry for 5 minutes. Carefully turn the gordita over and air-fry for an additional 5 minutes, until both sides are browned. When finished air frying all four gorditas, layer them back into the air fryer for an additional minute to make sure they are all warm before serving with sour cream and salsa.

Variations & Ingredients Tips:

- Use ground beef, chicken or turkey instead of pork
- Add some diced jalapeños or hot sauce to the meat mixture for spice
- Top with guacamole, diced onions and fresh cilantro

Per Serving: Calories: 925; Total Fat: 41g; Saturated Fat: 18g; Cholesterol: 121mg; Sodium: 1830mg; Total Carbs: 91g; Dietary Fiber: 14g; Total Sugars: 8g; Protein: 50g

Indonesian Pork Satay

Servings: 4 | Prep Time: 20 Minutes | Cooking Time: 30 Minutes

Ingredients:

- 450g pork tenderloin, cubed
- 1/4 cup minced onion
- 2 garlic cloves, minced
- 1 jalapeño pepper, minced
- 2 tbsp lime juice
- 2 tbsp coconut milk
- 1/2 tbsp ground coriander
- 1/2 tsp ground cumin
- 2 tbsp peanut butter
- 2 tsp curry powder

Directions:

1. Combine the pork, onion, garlic, jalapeño, lime juice, coconut milk, peanut butter, ground coriander, cumin, and curry powder in a bowl. Stir well and allow to marinate for 10 minutes.
2. Preheat air fryer to 380°F/193°C. Use a holey spoon and take the pork out of the marinade and set the marinade aside. Poke 8 bamboo skewers through the meat, then place the skewers in the air fryer. Use a cooking brush to rub the marinade on each skewer, then Grill for 10-14 minutes, adding more marinade if necessary. The pork should be golden and cooked through when finished. Serve warm.

Variations & Ingredients Tips:

- Use chicken instead of pork for chicken satay
- Add some brown sugar or honey to the marinade for a sweet and savory flavor
- Serve with peanut dipping sauce and cucumber salad on the side

Per Serving: Calories: 325; Total Fat: 14g; Saturated Fat: 4g; Cholesterol: 95mg; Sodium: 220mg; Total Carbs: 11g; Dietary Fiber: 2g; Total Sugars: 3g; Protein: 36g

Crispy Ham And Eggs

Servings: 3 | Prep Time: 5 Minutes | Cooking Time: 9 Minutes

Ingredients:

- 2 cups rice-puff cereal, such as Rice Krispies
- ¼ cup maple syrup
- 225 g ¼- to 1.3-cm-thick ham steak (gluten-free, if a concern)
- 1 tablespoon unsalted butter
- 3 large eggs
- ⅛ teaspoon table salt
- ⅛ teaspoon ground black pepper

Directions:

1. Preheat the air fryer to 200°C/400°F.
2. Pour the cereal into a food processor, cover, and process until finely ground. Pour the ground cereal into a shallow soup plate or a small pie plate.
3. Smear the maple syrup on both sides of the ham, then set the ham into the ground cereal. Turn a few times, pressing gently, until evenly coated.
4. Set the ham steak in the basket and air-fry undisturbed for 5 minutes, or until browned.
5. Meanwhile, melt the butter in a medium or large non-stick skillet set over medium heat. Crack the eggs into the skillet and cook until the whites are set and the yolks are hot, about 3 minutes (or 4 minutes for a more set yolk). Season with the salt and pepper.
6. When the ham is ready, transfer it to a serving platter, then slip the eggs from the skillet on top of it. Divide into portions to serve.

Variations & Ingredients Tips:

- Use different types of cereal, such as cornflakes or breadcrumbs, for a variety of textures.
- Add some chopped fresh herbs, such as parsley or chives, to the eggs for extra flavor.
- Serve the ham and eggs with a side of roasted potatoes or sliced tomatoes for a classic breakfast.

Per Serving: Calories: 330; Total Fat: 16g; Saturated Fat: 6g; Cholesterol: 255mg; Sodium: 1070mg; Total Carbs: 27g; Fiber: 0g; Sugars: 16g; Protein: 20g

Balsamic Marinated Rib Eye Steak With Balsamic Fried Cipollini Onions

Servings: 2 | Prep Time: 10 Minutes (plus Marinating Time) | Cooking Time: 22-26 Minutes

Ingredients:

- 3 tablespoons balsamic vinegar, divided
- 2 garlic cloves, sliced
- 1 tablespoon Dijon mustard
- 1 teaspoon fresh thyme leaves
- 1 (400g) boneless rib eye steak
- Coarsely ground black pepper
- Salt
- 227g bag cipollini onions, peeled

Directions:

1. Combine 3 tbsp vinegar, garlic, mustard and thyme. Pour over steak and pierce with a fork. Season generously with pepper.
2. Marinate steak 2-24 hours in the fridge. Let sit at room temp 30 mins before cooking.
3. Preheat air fryer to 200°C/400°F.
4. Season steak with salt and air fry for 12-16 mins, flipping halfway, until desired doneness.
5. Toss onions with 1 tsp vinegar and salt.
6. Remove steak and let rest. Air fry onions for 10 mins.
7. Slice steak and serve with fried onions on top.

Variations & Ingredients Tips:

- Use a different cut of steak like strip steak or tenderloin.
- Add other herbs like rosemary or oregano to the marinade.
- Toss the fried onions with a bit of balsamic glaze before serving.

Per Serving: Calories: 520; Total Fat: 32g; Saturated Fat: 13g; Cholesterol: 125mg; Sodium: 450mg; Total Carbohydrates: 14g; Dietary Fiber: 1g; Total Sugars: 9g; Protein: 41g

Crispy Pierogi With Kielbasa And Onions

Servings: 3 | Prep Time: 5 Minutes | Cooking Time: 20 Minutes

Ingredients:

- 6 frozen potato and cheese pierogi, thawed (about 12 pierogi to 450 g)
- 225 g smoked kielbasa, sliced into 1.25 cm thick rounds
- ¾ cup very roughly chopped sweet onion, preferably Vidalia
- Vegetable oil spray

Directions:

1. Preheat the air fryer to 190°C/375°F.
2. Put the pierogi, kielbasa rounds, and onion in a large bowl. Coat them with vegetable oil spray, toss well, spray again, and toss until everything is glistening.
3. When the machine is at temperature, dump the contents of the bowl it into the basket. (Items may be leaning against each other and even on top of each other.) Air-fry, tossing and rearranging everything twice so that all covered surfaces get exposed, for 20 minutes, or until the sausages have begun to brown and the pierogi are crisp.
4. Pour the contents of the basket onto a serving platter. Wait a minute or two just to take make sure nothing's searing hot before serving.

Variations & Ingredients Tips:

- Use different types of pierogi, such as sauerkraut or mushroom, for a variety of flavors.
- Add some sliced bell peppers or zucchini to the pierogi mixture for extra vegetables.
- Serve the pierogi with a side of sour cream or applesauce for a classic pairing.

Per Serving: Calories: 440; Total Fat: 26g; Saturated Fat: 9g; Cholesterol: 65mg; Sodium: 1120mg; Total Carbs: 35g; Fiber: 2g; Sugars: 5g; Protein: 17g

Berbere Beef Steaks

Servings: 4 | Prep Time: 15 Minutes | Cooking Time: 45 Minutes

Ingredients:

- 1 chipotle pepper in adobo sauce, minced
- 450 g skirt steak
- 2 tbsp chipotle sauce
- ¼ tsp Berbere seasoning
- Salt and pepper to taste

Directions:

1. Cut the steak into 4 equal pieces, then place them on a plate. Mix together chipotle pepper, adobo sauce, salt, pepper, and Berbere seasoning in a bowl. Spread the mixture on both sides of the steak. Chill for 2 hours. Preheat air fryer to 200°C/390°F. Place the steaks in the frying basket and bake for 5 minutes on each side for well-done meat. Allow the steaks to rest for 5 more minutes. To serve, slice against the grain.

Variations & Ingredients Tips:

- Use flank steak, sirloin, or ribeye instead of skirt steak for different cuts of beef.
- Add minced garlic, grated ginger, or chopped herbs to the spice rub for extra flavor.
- Serve with roasted vegetables, mashed potatoes, or a fresh salad for a complete meal.

Per Serving: Calories: 222; Total Fat: 12g; Saturated Fat: 5g; Cholesterol: 74mg; Sodium: 176mg; Total Carbohydrates: 1g; Dietary Fiber: 0g; Total Sugars: 0g; Protein: 25g

Fusion Tender Flank Steak

Servings: 4 | Prep Time: 15 Minutes | Cooking Time: 25 Minutes

Ingredients:

- 2 tbsp cilantro, chopped
- 2 tbsp chives, chopped
- ¼ tsp red pepper flakes
- 1 jalapeño pepper, minced
- 1 lime, juiced
- 3 tbsp olive oil
- Salt and pepper to taste
- 2 tbsp sesame oil
- 5 tbsp tamari sauce
- 3 tsp honey
- 1 tbsp grated fresh ginger
- 2 green onions, minced
- 2 garlic cloves, minced
- 567 g flank steak

Directions:

1. Combine the jalapeño pepper, cilantro, chives, lime juice, olive oil, salt, and pepper in a bowl. Set aside. Mix the sesame oil, tamari sauce, honey, ginger, green onions, garlic, and pepper flakes in another bowl. Stir until the honey is dissolved. Put the steak into the bowl and massage the marinade onto the meat. Marinate for 2 hours in the fridge. Preheat air fryer to 195°C/390°F.

2. Remove the steak from the marinade and place it in the greased frying basket. Air Fry for about 6 minutes, flip, and continue cooking for 6-8 more minutes. Allow to rest for a few minutes, slice thinly against the grain and top with the prepared dressing. Serve and enjoy!

Variations & Ingredients Tips:

- Swap the flank steak for skirt steak or hanger steak
- Add some sesame seeds to the dressing for crunch and nuttiness
- Serve with steamed rice and stir-fried vegetables for an Asian-inspired meal

Per Serving: Calories: 473; Total Fat: 32g; Saturated Fat: 7g; Cholesterol: 68mg; Sodium: 1590mg; Total Carbs: 13g; Dietary Fiber: 1g; Total Sugars: 9g; Protein: 36g

Tarragon Pork Tenderloin

Servings: 4 | Prep Time: 10 Minutes | Cooking Time: 25 Minutes

Ingredients:

- ½ teaspoon dried tarragon
- 454 g pork tenderloin, sliced
- Salt and pepper to taste
- 2 tablespoons Dijon mustard

- 1 clove garlic, minced
- 1 cup bread crumbs
- 2 tablespoons olive oil

Directions:

1. Preheat air fryer to 200°C/390°F. Using a rolling pin, pound the pork slices until they are about 2 cm thick. Season both sides with salt and pepper. Coat the pork with mustard and season with garlic and tarragon. In a shallow bowl, mix bread crumbs and olive oil. Dredge the pork with the bread crumbs, pressing firmly, so that it adheres. Put the pork in the frying basket and Air Fry until the pork outside is brown and crisp, 12-14 minutes. Serve warm.

Variations & Ingredients Tips:

- Substitute tarragon with thyme, rosemary or sage
- Use honey mustard or whole grain mustard instead of Dijon
- Serve with roasted potatoes, green beans or apple compote

Per Serving: Calories: 329; Total Fat: 14g; Saturated Fat: 3g; Cholesterol: 83mg; Sodium: 455mg; Total Carbs: 20g; Dietary Fiber: 1g; Total Sugars: 2g; Protein: 30g

Wiener Schnitzel

Servings: 4 | Prep Time: 10 Minutes | Cooking Time: 14 Minutes

Ingredients:

- 4 thin boneless pork loin chops
- 2 tablespoons lemon juice
- 1/2 cup all-purpose flour
- 1 teaspoon salt
- 1/4 teaspoon marjoram
- 1 cup plain breadcrumbs
- 2 large eggs, beaten
- Oil for misting or cooking spray

Directions:

1. Rub the lemon juice into all sides of pork chops.
2. Mix together the flour, salt, and marjoram. Place flour mixture on a sheet of wax paper.
3. Place breadcrumbs on another sheet of wax paper.
4. Dip pork chops in flour, then beaten eggs, then breadcrumbs, coating both sides. Mist all sides with oil or cooking spray.
5. Spray air fryer basket with nonstick spray and place breaded pork chops in basket.
6. Cook at 198°C/390°F for 7 minutes. Turn chops, mist again with oil, and cook for another 7 minutes until well done.
7. Serve with lemon wedges.

Variations & Ingredients Tips:

- Use panko breadcrumbs instead of regular for extra crunch
- Add grated parmesan or lemon zest to the breadcrumb mixture
- Pound the pork chops thin if they are not thin-cut

Per Serving: Calories: 385; Total Fat: 10g; Saturated Fat: 2g; Cholesterol: 165mg; Sodium: 725mg; Total Carbs: 45g; Dietary Fiber: 1g; Total Sugars: 2g; Protein: 28g

Asy Carnitas

Servings: 3 | Prep Time: 10 Minutes (plus Marinating Time) | Cooking Time: 25 Minutes

Ingredients:

- 680 g boneless country-style pork ribs, cut into 5 cm pieces
- ¼ cup orange juice
- 2 tablespoons brine from a jar of pickles, any type, even pickled jalapeño rings (gluten-free, if a concern)
- 2 teaspoons minced garlic
- 2 teaspoons minced fresh oregano leaves
- ¾ teaspoon ground cumin
- ¾ teaspoon table salt
- ¾ teaspoon ground black pepper

Directions:

1. Mix the country-style pork rib pieces, orange juice, pickle brine, garlic, oregano, cumin, salt, and pepper in a large bowl. Cover and refrigerate for at least 2 hours or up to 10 hours, stirring the mixture occasionally.
2. Preheat the air fryer to 200°C/400°F. Set the rib pieces in their bowl on the counter as the machine heats.
3. Use kitchen tongs to transfer the rib pieces to the basket, arranging them in one layer. Some may touch. Air-fry for 25 minutes, turning and rearranging the pieces at the 10- and 20-minute marks to make sure all surfaces have been exposed to the air currents, until browned and sizzling.
4. Use clean kitchen tongs to transfer the rib pieces to a wire rack. Cool for a couple of minutes before serving.

Variations & Ingredients Tips:

- Use different types of citrus juice, such as lemon or lime, for a variety of flavors.

- ▸ Add some minced onion or jalapeño to the marinade for extra flavor.
- ▸ Serve the carnitas with warm tortillas, salsa, and guacamole for a classic Mexican meal.

Per Serving: Calories: 480; Total Fat: 30g; Saturated Fat: 10g; Cholesterol: 165mg; Sodium: 970mg; Total Carbs: 5g; Fiber: 0g; Sugars: 3g; Protein: 45g

Delicious Juicy Pork Meatballs

Servings: 4 | Prep Time: 10 Minutes | Cooking Time: 35 Minutes

Ingredients:

- ¼ cup grated cheddar cheese
- 450 g ground pork
- 1 egg
- 1 tablespoon Greek yogurt
- ½ teaspoon onion powder
- ¼ cup chopped parsley
- 2 tablespoons bread crumbs
- ¼ teaspoon garlic powder
- Salt and pepper to taste

Directions:

1. Preheat air fryer to 180°C/350°F.
2. In a bowl, combine the ground pork, egg, yogurt, onion, parsley, cheddar cheese, bread crumbs, garlic, salt, and black pepper. Form mixture into 16 meatballs.
3. Place meatballs in the lightly greased frying basket and Air Fry for 8-10 minutes, flipping once.
4. Serve.

Variations & Ingredients Tips:

- ▸ Use different types of cheese, such as mozzarella or Parmesan, for a variety of flavors.
- ▸ Add some minced jalapeño or red pepper flakes to the meatball mixture for a spicy kick.
- ▸ Serve the meatballs with a side of tomato sauce or barbecue sauce for dipping.

Per Serving: Calories: 320; Total Fat: 22g; Saturated Fat: 9g; Cholesterol: 135mg; Sodium: 280mg; Total Carbs: 5g; Fiber: 0g; Sugars: 1g; Protein: 27g

Balsamic Beef & Veggie Skewers

Servings: 4 | Prep Time: 15 Minutes | Cooking Time: 25 Minutes

Ingredients:

- 2 tbsp balsamic vinegar
- 2 tsp olive oil
- 1/2 tsp dried oregano
- Salt and pepper to taste
- 340g round steak, cubed
- 1 red bell pepper, sliced
- 1 yellow bell pepper, sliced
- 1 cup cherry tomatoes

Directions:

1. Preheat air fryer to 199°C/390°F.
2. In a bowl, mix balsamic vinegar, olive oil, oregano, salt and pepper.
3. Add steak cubes and toss to coat. Marinate for 10 minutes.
4. Thread steak, bell peppers and tomatoes onto 8 metal skewers, alternating ingredients.
5. Place skewers in air fryer basket in a single layer.
6. Air fry for 5-7 minutes, turning once, until steak is cooked through and veggies are tender.
7. Serve immediately.

Variations & Ingredients Tips:

- ▸ Use chicken or shrimp instead of beef.
- ▸ Add mushrooms, zucchini or onions to the skewers.
- ▸ Brush with reserved marinade halfway through cooking.

Per Serving: Calories: 170; Total Fat: 7g; Saturated Fat: 2g; Cholesterol: 50mg; Sodium: 65mg; Total Carbohydrates: 6g; Dietary Fiber: 1g; Total Sugars: 4g; Protein: 19g

Tex-mex Beef Carnitas

Servings: 4 | Prep Time: 15 Minutes | Cooking Time: 30 Minutes

Ingredients:

- 567g flank steak, cut into 2.5cm strips
- 1 1/2 cups grated Colby cheese
- Salt and pepper to taste
- 2 tbsp lime juice
- 4 garlic cloves, minced
- 2 tsp chipotle powder
- 1 red bell pepper, sliced
- 1 yellow bell pepper, sliced
- 1 tbsp chili oil
- 1/2 cup salsa
- 8 corn tortillas

Directions:

1. Preheat the air fryer to 400°F/205°C. Lay the strips in a bowl and sprinkle with salt, pepper, lime juice, garlic, and chipotle powder. Toss well and let marinate. In the frying basket, combine the bell peppers and chili oil and toss.
2. Air Fry for 6 minutes or until crispy but tender. Drain the steak and discard the liquid. Lay the steak in the basket on top of the peppers and fry for 7-9 minutes more until browned. Divide the strips among tortillas and top with pepper strips, salsa, and cheese. Fold and serve.

Variations & Ingredients Tips:

- Use skirt or flank steak instead of flank steak
- Add sliced onions or jalapeños to the pepper mix
- Substitute cotija or queso fresco for the Colby cheese

Per Serving: Calories: 620; Total Fat: 29g; Saturated Fat: 12g; Cholesterol: 100mg; Sodium: 670mg; Total Carbs: 44g; Dietary Fiber: 5g; Total Sugars: 5g; Protein: 45g

Steak Fajitas

Servings: 4 | Prep Time: 15 Minutes | Cooking Time: 20 Minutes

Ingredients:

- 454 g beef flank steak, cut into strips
- 1 red bell pepper, cut into strips
- 1 green bell pepper, cut into strips
- 118 g sweet corn
- 1 shallot, cut into strips
- 2 tablespoons fajita seasoning
- Salt and pepper to taste
- 2 tablespoons olive oil
- 8 flour tortillas

Directions:

1. Preheat air fryer to 190°C/380°F. Combine beef, bell peppers, corn, shallot, fajita seasoning, salt, pepper, and olive oil in a large bowl until well mixed.
2. Pour the beef and vegetable mixture into the air fryer. Air Fry for 9-11 minutes, shaking the basket once halfway through. Spoon a portion of the beef and vegetables in each of the tortillas and top with favorite toppings. Serve.

Variations & Ingredients Tips:

- Use chicken breast or shrimp instead of steak for a change
- Add some sliced jalapeños or hot sauce for spicy kick
- Serve with guacamole, sour cream, salsa and lime wedges

Per Serving: Calories: 514; Total Fat: 22g; Saturated Fat: 6g; Cholesterol: 68mg; Sodium: 1007mg; Total Carbs: 49g; Dietary Fiber: 4g; Total Sugars: 4g; Protein: 32g

Kentucky-style Pork Tenderloin

Servings: 2 | Prep Time: 10 Minutes | Cooking Time: 30 Minutes

Ingredients:

- 454g pork tenderloin, halved crosswise
- 1 tbsp smoked paprika
- 2 tsp ground cumin
- 1 tsp garlic powder
- 1 tsp shallot powder
- 1/4 tsp chili pepper
- Salt and pepper to taste
- 1 tsp Italian seasoning
- 2 tbsp butter, melted
- 1 tsp Worcestershire sauce

Directions:

1. Preheat air fryer to 350°F/177°C. In a shallow bowl, combine all spices. Set aside. In another bowl, whisk butter and Worcestershire sauce and brush over pork tenderloin. Sprinkle with the seasoning mix. Place pork in the lightly greased frying basket and Air Fry for 16 minutes, flipping once. Let sit onto a cutting board for 5 minutes before slicing. Serve immediately.

Variations & Ingredients Tips:

- Use smoked paprika or chipotle powder for a smoky flavor
- Add brown sugar or honey to the spice rub for a sweet-spicy glaze
- Brush tenderloin with mustard before applying rub for extra tang

Per Serving: Calories: 375; Total Fat: 16g; Saturated Fat: 7g; Cholesterol: 145mg; Sodium: 580mg; Total Carbs: 7g; Dietary Fiber: 2g; Total Sugars: 2g; Protein: 48g

Calf's Liver

Servings: 4 | Prep Time: 10 Minutes | Cooking Time: 5 Minutes

Ingredients:

- 450-g sliced calf's liver
- Salt and pepper
- 2 eggs
- 2 tablespoons milk
- 1/2 cup whole wheat flour
- 1 1/2 cups panko breadcrumbs
- 1/2 cup plain breadcrumbs
- 1/2 teaspoon salt
- 1/4 teaspoon pepper
- Oil for misting or cooking spray

Directions:

1. Cut liver slices crosswise into strips about 25cm wide. Sprinkle with salt and pepper to taste.
2. Beat together egg and milk in a shallow dish.
3. Place wheat flour in a second shallow dish.
4. In a third shallow dish, mix together panko, plain breadcrumbs, 1/2 teaspoon salt, and 1/4 teaspoon pepper.
5. Preheat air fryer to 390°F/199°C.
6. Dip liver strips in flour, egg wash, and then breadcrumbs, pressing in coating slightly to make crumbs stick.
7. Cooking half the liver at a time, place strips in air fryer basket in a single layer, close but not touching. Cook at 390°F/199°C for 5 minutes or until done to your preference.
8. Repeat step 7 to cook remaining liver.

Variations & Ingredients Tips:

- For extra crunch, use all panko breadcrumbs instead of a mix
- Add cayenne pepper or Cajun seasoning to the breadcrumb mix for a kick of flavor
- Serve with lemon wedges for squeezing over the cooked liver

Per Serving: Calories: 276; Total Fat: 8g; Saturated Fat: 2g; Cholesterol: 284mg; Sodium: 620mg; Total Carbs: 27g; Dietary Fiber: 2g; Total Sugars: 1g; Protein: 23g

Horseradish Mustard Pork Chops

Servings: 2 | Prep Time: 10 Minutes | Cooking Time: 20 Minutes

Ingredients:

- 50 g grated Pecorino cheese
- 1 egg white
- 1 tbsp horseradish mustard
- ¼ tsp black pepper
- 2 pork chops
- ¼ cup chopped cilantro

Directions:

1. Preheat air fryer to 175°C/350°F. Whisk egg white and horseradish mustard in a bowl. In another bowl, combine Pecorino cheese and black pepper. Dip pork chops in the mustard mixture, then dredge them in the Parmesan mixture. Place pork chops in the frying basket lightly greased with olive oil and Air Fry for 12-14 minutes until cooked through and tender, flipping twice. Transfer the chops to a cutting board and let sit for 5 minutes. Scatter with cilantro to serve.

Variations & Ingredients Tips:

- Substitute Pecorino with Parmesan or Asiago cheese
- Use Dijon or whole grain mustard instead of horseradish
- Serve with roasted potatoes and steamed green beans

Per Serving: Calories: 328; Total Fat: 18g; Saturated Fat: 7g; Cholesterol: 100mg; Sodium: 555mg; Total Carbs: 1g; Dietary Fiber: 0g; Total Sugars: 0g; Protein: 40g

Cajun Pork Loin Chops

Servings: 4 | Prep Time: 20 Minutes | Cooking Time: 25 Minutes

Ingredients:

- 8 thin boneless pork loin chops (около 680g total)
- 3.75ml Coarse sea salt
- 1 egg, beaten
- 5ml Cajun seasoning
- 120g bread crumbs
- 1 cucumber, sliced
- 1 tomato, sliced

Directions:

1. Place the chops between two sheets of parchment paper. Pound the pork to 6mm thickness using a meat mallet or rolling pin. Season with sea salt. In a shallow bowl, beat the egg with 5ml of water and Cajun seasoning. In a second bowl, add the breadcrumbs. Dip the chops into the egg mixture, shake, and dip into the crumbs.
2. Preheat air fryer to 400°F/205°C. Place the chops in the greased frying basket and Air Fry for 6-8 minutes, flipping once until golden and cooked through. Serve immediately with cucumber and tomato.

Variations & Ingredients Tips:

▶ Use panko breadcrumbs instead of regular for an extra crispy coating
▶ Make a remoulade or comeback sauce for dipping
▶ Let the breaded chops rest for 10 minutes before frying for a better crust

Per Serving: Calories: 250; Total Fat: 8g; Saturated Fat: 2.5g; Cholesterol: 135mg; Sodium: 540mg; Total Carbs: 15g; Fiber: 1g; Sugars: 1g; Protein: 29g

Fish And Seafood Recipes

Hazelnut-crusted Fish

Servings: 4 | Prep Time: 10 Minutes | Cooking Time: 30 Minutes

Ingredients:

- 1/2 cup hazelnuts, ground
- 1 scallion, finely chopped
- 1 lemon, juiced and zested
- 1/2 tbsp olive oil
- Salt and pepper to taste
- 3 skinless sea bass fillets
- 1 tsp Dijon mustard

Directions:

1. Mix hazelnuts, scallion, lemon zest, oil, salt and pepper in a bowl.
2. Spray tops of fish with cooking oil and squeeze lemon juice over them.
3. Coat tops with mustard, then hazelnut mixture, pressing gently to adhere.
4. Preheat air fryer to 190°C/375°F.
5. Air fry fish for 7-8 mins until browned and cooked through.
6. Serve hot.

Variations & Ingredients Tips:

▶ Use other nuts like almonds or pecans for the crust.
▶ Mix panko breadcrumbs into the nut crust for extra crunch.
▶ Add parmesan or herbs to the crust mixture.

Per Serving: Calories: 248; Total Fat: 13g; Saturated Fat: 2g; Cholesterol: 54mg; Sodium: 237mg; Total Carbs: 8g; Dietary Fiber: 2g; Total Sugars: 1g; Protein: 26g

Tuna Nuggets In Hoisin Sauce

Servings: 4 | Prep Time: 10 Minutes | Cooking Time: 7 Minutes

Ingredients:

- 1/2 cup hoisin sauce
- 2 tablespoons rice wine vinegar
- 2 teaspoons sesame oil
- 1 teaspoon garlic powder
- 2 teaspoons dried lemongrass
- 1/4 teaspoon red pepper flakes
- 1/2 small onion, quartered and thinly sliced
- 225g fresh tuna, cut into 2.5-cm cubes
- Cooking spray
- 3 cups cooked jasmine rice

Directions:

1. Mix the hoisin sauce, vinegar, sesame oil, and seasonings together.
2. Stir in the onions and tuna nuggets.
3. Spray air fryer baking pan with nonstick spray and pour in tuna mixture.
4. Cook at 200°C/390°F for 3 minutes. Stir gently.
5. Cook 2 minutes and stir again, checking for doneness. Tuna should be barely cooked through, just beginning to flake and still very moist. If necessary, continue cooking and stirring in 1-minute intervals until done.
6. Serve warm over hot jasmine rice.

Variations & Ingredients Tips:

- Use salmon, swordfish or shrimp instead of tuna.
- Add some diced bell peppers or carrots to the mix.
- Serve over rice noodles or in lettuce wraps.

Per Serving: Calories: 350; Total Fat: 6g; Saturated Fat: 1g; Cholesterol: 30mg; Sodium: 950mg; Total Carbs: 54g; Dietary Fiber: 2g; Total Sugars: 13g; Protein: 22g

Black Olive & Shrimp Salad

Servings: 4 | Prep Time: 10 Minutes | Cooking Time: 15 Minutes

Ingredients:

- 450g cleaned shrimp, deveined
- ½ cup olive oil
- 4 garlic cloves, minced
- 1 tbsp balsamic vinegar
- 1/4 tsp cayenne pepper
- 1/4 tsp dried basil
- 1/4 tsp salt
- 1/4 tsp onion powder
- 1 tomato, diced
- ¼ cup black olives

Directions:

1. Preheat air fryer to 190°C/380°F.
2. Place the olive oil, garlic, balsamic, cayenne, basil, onion powder and salt in a bowl and stir to combine.
3. Divide the tomatoes and black olives between 4 small ramekins. Top with shrimp and pour a quarter of the oil mixture over the shrimp.
4. Bake for 6-8 minutes until the shrimp are cooked through.
5. Serve.

Variations & Ingredients Tips:

- Use kalamata olives or green olives stuffed with garlic or almonds.
- Add some crumbled feta cheese or fresh mozzarella balls.
- Serve over mixed greens or couscous.

Per Serving: Calories: 330; Total Fat: 27g; Saturated Fat: 4g; Cholesterol: 180mg; Sodium: 460mg; Total Carbs: 4g; Dietary Fiber: 1g; Total Sugars: 2g; Protein: 21g

Cajun-seasoned Shrimp

Servings: 2 | Prep Time: 5 Minutes | Cooking Time: 15 Minutes

Ingredients:

- 454 grams shelled tail on shrimp, deveined
- 2 tsp grated Parmesan cheese
- 2 tbsp butter, melted
- 1 tsp cayenne pepper
- 1 tsp garlic powder
- 2 tsp Cajun seasoning
- 1 tbsp lemon juice

Directions:

1. Preheat air fryer at 180°C/350°F.
2. Toss the shrimp, melted butter, cayenne pepper, garlic powder and cajun seasoning in a bowl, place them in the greased air fryer basket, and Air Fry for 6 minutes, flipping once.
3. Transfer it to a plate. Squeeze lemon juice over shrimp and stir in Parmesan cheese.
4. Serve immediately.

Variations & Ingredients Tips:

- Use peeled, deveined shrimp with or without tails for easier eating.
- Add a dash of hot sauce or red pepper flakes for extra heat.
- Serve over rice, pasta, or in tacos or po' boy sandwiches.

Per Serving: Calories: 400; Total Fat: 22g; Saturated Fat: 12g; Sodium: 2040mg; Total Carbohydrates: 4g; Dietary Fiber: 1g; Total Sugars: 0g; Protein: 45g

Sriracha Salmon Melt Sandwiches

Servings: 4 | Prep Time: 10 Minutes | Cooking Time: 20 Minutes

Ingredients:

- 2 tbsp butter, softened
- 2 (210g) cans pink salmon
- 2 English muffins
- 1/3 cup mayonnaise
- 2 tbsp Dijon mustard
- 1 tbsp fresh lemon juice
- 1/3 cup chopped celery
- 1/2 tsp sriracha sauce
- 4 slices tomato
- 4 slices Swiss cheese

Directions:

1. Preheat air fryer to 190°C/370°F.
2. Split muffins and spread with butter. Toast in air fryer 3-5 mins until golden.
3. Mix salmon, mayo, mustard, lemon, celery and sriracha.
4. Top muffin halves with salmon mixture, tomato and cheese.
5. Air fry sandwiches 4-6 minutes until cheese melts.
6. Serve hot.

Variations & Ingredients Tips:

- Use canned tuna or crab meat instead of salmon.
- Add diced onion, pickles or jalapeño to the filling.
- Brush muffins with garlic butter before toasting.

Per Serving: Calories: 430; Total Fat: 30g; Saturated Fat: 10g; Cholesterol: 95mg; Sodium: 780mg; Total Carbs: 18g; Dietary Fiber: 2g; Sugars: 4g; Protein: 23g

Fish Piccata With Crispy Potatoes

Servings: 4 | Prep Time: 15 Minutes | Cooking Time: 30 Minutes

Ingredients:

- 4 cod fillets
- 1 tbsp butter
- 2 tsp capers
- 1 garlic clove, minced
- 2 tbsp lemon juice
- 450g asparagus, trimmed
- 450g potatoes, cubed
- 1 tbsp olive oil
- Salt and pepper to taste
- 1/4 tsp garlic powder
- 1 tsp dried rosemary
- 1 tsp dried parsley
- 1 tsp chopped dill

Directions:

1. Preheat air fryer to 195°C/380°F.
2. Place each fillet on foil. Top with butter, capers, dill, garlic and lemon juice. Seal pouches.
3. Toss asparagus, potatoes, oil, spices and seasoning.
4. Air fry asparagus for 4 mins, shake basket.
5. Top with fish pouches and roast 8 more mins.
6. Let stand 5 mins before serving.

Variations & Ingredients Tips:

- Use halibut, tilapia or sole fillets instead of cod.
- Toss potatoes with Parmesan or ranch seasoning before roasting.
- Add sliced lemon or caramelized onions to the fish packets.

Per Serving: Calories: 265; Total Fat: 7g; Saturated Fat: 2g; Cholesterol: 60mg; Sodium: 214mg; Total Carbs: 30g; Dietary Fiber: 5g; Total Sugars: 2g; Protein: 22g

The Best Shrimp Risotto

Servings: 4 | Prep Time: 20 Minutes | Cooking Time: 50 Minutes + 5 Minutes To Sit

Ingredients:

- 1/3 cup grated Parmesan
- 2 tbsp olive oil
- 450g peeled shrimp, deveined
- 1 onion, chopped
- 1 red bell pepper, chopped
- Salt and pepper to taste
- 1 cup Carnaroli rice
- 2 1/3 cups vegetable stock
- 2 tbsp butter
- 1 tbsp heavy cream

Directions:

1. Preheat the air fryer to 190°C/380°F.
2. Add a tbsp of olive oil to a cake pan, then toss in the shrimp. Put the pan in the frying basket and cook the shrimp for 4-7 minutes or until they curl and pinken. Remove the shrimp and set aside.
3. Add the other tbsp of olive oil to the cake pan, then add the onion, bell pepper, salt, and pepper and Air Fry for 3 minutes.
4. Add the rice to the cake pan, stir, and cook for 2 minutes. Add the stock, stir again, and cover the pan with foil. Bake for another 18-22 minutes, stirring twice until the rice is tender.
5. Remove the foil. Return the shrimp to the pan along with butter, heavy cream, and Parmesan, then cook for another minute.
6. Stir and serve.

Variations & Ingredients Tips:

- Use chicken stock or seafood stock instead of vegetable for more flavor.
- Add some saffron threads or turmeric for color and aroma.
- Garnish with chopped parsley, basil or chives before serving.

Per Serving: Calories: 440; Total Fat: 20g; Saturated Fat:

8g; Cholesterol: 210mg; Sodium: 800mg; Total Carbs: 40g; Dietary Fiber: 2g; Total Sugars: 4g; Protein: 29g

Cheesy Salmon-stuffed Avocados

Servings: 2 | Prep Time: 15 Minutes | Cooking Time: 20 Minutes

Ingredients:

- ¼ cup apple cider vinegar
- 1 tsp granular sugar
- ¼ cup sliced red onions
- 57 grams cream cheese, softened
- 1 tbsp capers
- 2 halved avocados, pitted
- 113 grams smoked salmon
- ¼ tsp dried dill
- 2 cherry tomatoes, halved
- 1 tbsp cilantro, chopped

Directions:

1. Warm apple vinegar and sugar in a saucepan over medium heat and simmer for 4 minutes until boiling. Add in onion and turn the heat off. Let sit until ready to use. Drain before using.
2. In a small bowl, combine cream cheese and capers. Let chill in the fridge until ready to use.
3. Preheat air fryer to 180°C/350°F.
4. Place avocado halves, cut sides-up, in the air fryer basket, and Air Fry for 4 minutes. Transfer avocado halves to 2 plates.
5. Top with cream cheese mixture, smoked salmon, dill, red onions, tomato halves and cilantro.
6. Serve immediately.

Variations & Ingredients Tips:

- Use canned tuna, crab meat, or shrimp instead of smoked salmon.
- Add a squeeze of lemon juice or hot sauce to the cream cheese mixture for extra tang and spice.
- Serve on a bed of mixed greens or stuffed in a hollowed out tomato or bell pepper.

Per Serving: Calories: 450; Total Fat: 37g; Saturated Fat: 13g; Sodium: 860mg; Total Carbohydrates: 18g; Dietary Fiber: 9g; Total Sugars: 6g; Protein: 18g

Garlic-butter Lobster Tails

Servings: 2 | Prep Time: 5 Minutes | Cooking Time: 20 Minutes

Ingredients:

- 2 lobster tails
- 1 tbsp butter, melted
- 1/2 tsp Old Bay Seasoning
- 1/2 tsp garlic powder
- 1 tbsp chopped parsley
- 2 lemon wedges

Directions:

1. Preheat air fryer to 200°C/400°F.
2. Using kitchen shears, cut down the middle of each lobster tail on the softer side. Carefully run your finger between the lobster meat and the shell to loosen the meat.
3. Place lobster tails in the frying basket, cut sides up, and Air Fry for 4 minutes.
4. Rub with butter, garlic powder and Old Bay seasoning and cook for 4 more minutes.
5. Garnish with parsley and lemon wedges. Serve and enjoy!

Variations & Ingredients Tips:

- Add a pinch of cayenne or red pepper flakes for heat.
- Brush with a mixture of melted butter, lemon juice and Dijon mustard.
- Serve with drawn butter and steamed vegetables.

Per Serving: Calories: 180; Total Fat: 8g; Saturated Fat: 4.5g; Cholesterol: 130mg; Sodium: 690mg; Total Carbs: 2g; Dietary Fiber: 0g; Total Sugars: 0g; Protein: 24g

Easy Scallops With Lemon Butter

Servings: 3 | Prep Time: 5 Minutes | Cooking Time: 4 Minutes

Ingredients:

- 1 tablespoon olive oil
- 2 teaspoons minced garlic
- 1 teaspoon finely grated lemon zest
- 1/2 teaspoon red pepper flakes
- 1/4 teaspoon table salt
- 450g sea scallops
- 3 tablespoons butter, melted
- 1 1/2 tablespoons lemon juice

Directions:

1. Preheat the air fryer to 200°C/400°F.
2. Gently stir the olive oil, garlic, lemon zest, red pepper flakes, and salt in a bowl. Add the scallops and stir very gently until they are evenly and well coated.

3. When the machine is at temperature, arrange the scallops in a single layer in the basket. Some may touch. Air-fry undisturbed for 4 minutes, or until the scallops are opaque and firm.
4. While the scallops cook, stir the melted butter and lemon juice in a serving bowl. When the scallops are ready, pour them from the basket into this bowl. Toss well before serving.

Variations & Ingredients Tips:

- Add some capers, diced tomatoes or chopped parsley to the sauce.
- Use lime juice and cilantro instead of lemon and parsley for a Mexican twist.
- Serve over angel hair pasta, risotto or sautéed spinach.

Per Serving: Calories: 330; Total Fat: 21g; Saturated Fat: 10g; Cholesterol: 110mg; Sodium: 940mg; Total Carbs: 4g; Dietary Fiber: 0g; Total Sugars: 0g; Protein: 31g

Holiday Lobster Salad

Servings: 2 | Prep Time: 10 Minutes | Cooking Time: 20 Minutes

Ingredients:

- 2 lobster tails
- 1/4 cup mayonnaise
- 2 tsp lemon juice
- 1 stalk celery, sliced
- 2 tsp chopped chives
- 2 tsp chopped tarragon
- Salt and pepper to taste
- 2 tomato slices
- 4 cucumber slices
- 1 avocado, diced

Directions:

1. Preheat air fryer to 200°C/400°F.
2. Using kitchen shears, cut down the middle of each lobster tail on the softer side. Carefully run your finger between the lobster meat and the shell to loosen meat.
3. Place lobster tails, cut sides up, in the frying basket, and Air Fry for 8 minutes. Transfer to a large plate and let cool for 3 minutes until easy to handle, then pull lobster meat from the shell and roughly chop it.
4. Combine chopped lobster, mayonnaise, lemon juice, celery, chives, tarragon, salt, and pepper in a bowl.
5. Divide between 2 medium plates and top with tomato slices, cucumber and avocado cubes.
6. Serve immediately.

Variations & Ingredients Tips:

- Substitute lobster with crab, shrimp or crayfish.
- Add some diced red onion or fennel for crunch.
- Serve in lettuce cups, avocado halves or toasted rolls.

Per Serving: Calories: 440; Total Fat: 35g; Saturated Fat: 5g; Cholesterol: 130mg; Sodium: 620mg; Total Carbs: 12g; Dietary Fiber: 6g; Total Sugars: 3g; Protein: 24g

Almond-crusted Fish

Servings: 4 | Prep Time: 15 Minutes | Cooking Time: 10 Minutes

Ingredients:

- 4 (115-g) fish fillets
- 3/4 cup breadcrumbs
- 1/4 cup sliced almonds, crushed
- 2 tablespoons lemon juice
- 1/8 teaspoon cayenne
- Salt and pepper
- 3/4 cup flour
- 1 egg, beaten with 1 tablespoon water
- Oil for misting or cooking spray

Directions:

1. Split fish fillets lengthwise down the center to create 8 pieces.
2. Mix breadcrumbs and almonds together and set aside.
3. Mix the lemon juice and cayenne together. Brush on all sides of fish.
4. Season fish to taste with salt and pepper.
5. Place the flour on a sheet of wax paper.
6. Roll fillets in flour, dip in egg wash, and roll in the crumb mixture.
7. Mist both sides of fish with oil or cooking spray.
8. Spray air fryer basket and lay fillets inside.
9. Cook at 200°C/390°F for 5 minutes, turn fish over, and cook for an additional 5 minutes or until fish is done and flakes easily.

Variations & Ingredients Tips:

- Use panko breadcrumbs for extra crunch.
- Substitute almonds with pecans, walnuts or pistachios.
- Serve with tartar sauce and lemon wedges.

Per Serving: Calories: 270; Total Fat: 9g; Saturated Fat: 1.5g; Cholesterol: 110mg; Sodium: 320mg; Total Carbs: 22g; Dietary Fiber: 2g; Total Sugars: 1g; Protein: 25g

Sea Bass With Fruit Salsa

Servings: 4 | Prep Time: 15 Minutes | Cooking Time: 30 Minutes

Ingredients:

- 3 halved nectarines, pitted
- 4 sea bass fillets
- 2 tsp olive oil
- 3 plums, halved and pitted
- 1 cup red grapes
- 1 tbsp lemon juice
- 1 tbsp honey
- 1/2 tsp dried thyme

Directions:

1. Preheat air fryer to 200°C/390°F.
2. Lay sea bass fillets in frying basket, spritz with olive oil. Air Fry 4 minutes.
3. Remove basket, add nectarines, plums, grapes. Spritz with lemon juice, honey and thyme.
4. Return basket to fryer and Bake 5-9 more minutes until fish flakes and fruit is soft.
5. Serve hot.

Variations & Ingredients Tips:

- Use other fruits like pineapple, mango or strawberries.
- Add jalapeño or red onion to the salsa.
- Squeeze lime juice over the top before serving.

Per Serving: Calories: 220; Total Fat: 4g; Saturated Fat: 1g; Cholesterol: 65mg; Sodium: 65mg; Total Carbs: 25g; Dietary Fiber: 3g; Sugars: 18g; Protein: 22g

Fish Nuggets With Broccoli Dip

Servings: 4 | Prep Time: 20 Minutes | Cooking Time: 40 Minutes

Ingredients:

- 450g cod fillets, cut into chunks
- 1 1/2 cups broccoli florets
- 1/4 cup grated Parmesan
- 3 garlic cloves, peeled
- 3 tbsp sour cream
- 2 tbsp lemon juice
- 2 tbsp olive oil
- 2 egg whites
- 1 cup panko bread crumbs
- 1 tsp dried dill
- Salt and pepper to taste

Directions:

1. Preheat the air fryer to 200°C/400°F.
2. Put the broccoli and garlic in the greased frying basket and Air Fry for 5-7 minutes or until tender. Remove to a blender and add sour cream, lemon juice, olive oil, and 1/2 tsp of salt and process until smooth. Set the sauce aside.
3. Beat the egg whites until frothy in a shallow bowl. On a plate, combine the panko, Parmesan, dill, pepper, and the remaining 1/2 tsp of salt.
4. Dip the cod fillets in the egg whites, then the breadcrumbs, pressing to coat. Put half the cubes in the frying basket and spray with cooking oil.
5. Air Fry for 6-8 minutes or until the fish is cooked through.
6. Serve the fish with the sauce and enjoy!

Variations & Ingredients Tips:

- Use salmon, pollack or tilapia instead of cod.
- Add some cayenne or smoked paprika to the breading for a kick.
- Serve with sweet potato fries and lemon wedges.

Per Serving: Calories: 350; Total Fat: 15g; Saturated Fat: 5g; Cholesterol: 85mg; Sodium: 540mg; Total Carbs: 22g; Dietary Fiber: 3g; Total Sugars: 3g; Protein: 34g

Beer-breaded Halibut Fish Tacos

Servings: 4 | Prep Time: 40 Minutes | Cooking Time: 10 Minutes

Ingredients:

- 450g halibut, cut into 2.5-cm strips
- 1 cup light beer
- 1 jalapeño, minced and divided
- 1 clove garlic, minced
- 1/4 teaspoon ground cumin
- ½ cup cornmeal
- ¼ cup all-purpose flour
- 1¼ teaspoons sea salt, divided
- 2 cups shredded cabbage
- 1 lime, juiced and divided
- ¼ cup Greek yogurt
- ¼ cup Greek yogurt
- 1 cup grape tomatoes, quartered
- ½ cup chopped cilantro
- ¼ cup chopped onion
- 1 egg, whisked

- 8 corn tortillas

Directions:

1. In a shallow baking dish, place the fish, the beer, 1 teaspoon of the minced jalapeño, the garlic, and the cumin. Cover and refrigerate for 30 minutes.
2. Meanwhile, in a medium bowl, mix together the cornmeal, flour, and 1/2 teaspoon of the salt.
3. In large bowl, mix together the shredded cabbage, 1 tablespoon of the lime juice, the Greek yogurt, the mayonnaise, and 1/2 teaspoon of the salt.
4. In a small bowl, make the pico de gallo by mixing together the tomatoes, cilantro, onion, 1/4 teaspoon of the salt, the remaining jalapeño, and the remaining lime juice.
5. Remove the fish from the refrigerator and discard the marinade. Dredge the fish in the whisked egg; then dredge the fish in the cornmeal flour mixture, until all pieces of fish have been breaded.
6. Preheat the air fryer to 175°C/350°F.
7. Place the fish in the air fryer basket and spray liberally with cooking spray. Cook for 6 minutes, flip and shake the fish, and cook another 4 minutes.
8. While the fish is cooking, heat the tortillas in a heavy skillet for 1 to 2 minutes over high heat.
9. To assemble the tacos, place the battered fish on the heated tortillas, and top with slaw and pico de gallo. Serve immediately.

Variations & Ingredients Tips:

- Use cod, tilapia or snapper instead of halibut.
- Substitute the beer with sparkling water or ginger ale for a non-alcoholic version.
- Add some sliced avocado or guacamole on top.

Per Serving: Calories: 420; Total Fat: 18g; Saturated Fat: 4g; Cholesterol: 120mg; Sodium: 910mg; Total Carbs: 37g; Dietary Fiber: 5g; Total Sugars: 5g; Protein: 29g

Kid's Flounder Fingers

Servings: 4 | Prep Time: 10 Minutes | Cooking Time: 45 Minutes

Ingredients:

- 450g catfish flounder fillets, cut into 2.5cm chunks
- 1/2 cup seasoned fish fry breading mix

Directions:

1. Preheat air fryer to 200°C/400°F.
2. In a resealable bag, add flounder chunks and breading mix.
3. Seal and shake bag until fish is coated.
4. Place coated nuggets in a single layer in greased air fryer basket.
5. Air fry for 18-20 minutes, shaking basket once, until crisp.
6. Serve warm.

Variations & Ingredients Tips:

- Use any firm white fish like cod or haddock.
- Make your own seasoned breadcrumb mix with spices.
- Serve with tartar sauce, ketchup or ranch for dipping.

Per Serving: Calories: 167; Total Fat: 2g; Saturated Fat: 0g; Cholesterol: 51mg; Sodium: 513mg; Total Carbs: 13g; Dietary Fiber: 0g; Total Sugars: 1g; Protein: 23g

Masala Fish `n` Chips

Servings: 4 | Prep Time: 15 Minutes | Cooking Time: 30 Minutes

Ingredients:

- 2 russet potatoes, cut into strips
- 4 pollock fillets
- Salt and pepper to taste
- 1/2 tsp garam masala
- 1 egg white
- 3/4 cup bread crumbs
- 2 tbsp olive oil

Directions:

1. Preheat air fryer to 200°C/400°F.
2. Sprinkle the pollock fillets with salt, pepper, and garam masala.
3. In a shallow bowl, beat egg whites until foamy. In a separate bowl, stir together bread crumbs and 1 tablespoon olive oil until completely combined.
4. Dip the fillets into the egg white, then coat with the bread crumbs.
5. In a bowl, toss the potato strips with 1 tbsp olive oil. Place them in the frying basket and Air Fry for 10 minutes.
6. Slide-out the basket, shake the chips and place a metal holder over them. Arrange the fish fillets on the metal holder and cook for 10-12 minutes, flipping once.
7. Serve warm.

Variations & Ingredients Tips:

- Use other white fish like cod or tilapia.
- Add lemon juice or other spices to the egg wash.

> Serve with malt vinegar and tartar sauce for dipping.

Per Serving: Calories: 360; Total Fat: 13g; Saturated Fat: 2g; Cholesterol: 60mg; Sodium: 430mg; Total Carbs: 38g; Dietary Fiber: 3g; Total Sugars: 2g; Protein: 23g

Crab Cakes

Servings: 2 | Prep Time: 20 Minutes | Cooking Time: 10 Minutes

Ingredients:

- 1 teaspoon butter
- 1/3 cup finely diced onion
- 1/3 cup finely diced celery
- 1/4 cup mayonnaise
- 1 teaspoon Dijon mustard
- 1 egg
- Pinch ground cayenne pepper
- 1 teaspoon salt
- Freshly ground black pepper
- 450g lump crabmeat
- 1/2 cup + 2 tablespoons panko breadcrumbs, divided

Directions:

1. Melt the butter in a skillet over medium heat. Sauté the onion and celery until it starts to soften, but not brown – about 4 minutes. Transfer the cooked vegetables to a large bowl.
2. Add the mayonnaise, Dijon mustard, egg, cayenne pepper, salt and freshly ground black pepper to the bowl. Gently fold in the lump crabmeat and 2 tablespoons of panko breadcrumbs. Stir carefully so you don't break up all the crab pieces.
3. Preheat the air fryer to 200°C/400°F.
4. Place the remaining panko breadcrumbs in a shallow dish. Divide the crab mixture into 4 portions and shape each portion into a round patty. Dredge the crab patties in the breadcrumbs, coating both sides as well as the edges with the crumbs.
5. Air-fry the crab cakes for 5 minutes. Using a flat spatula, gently turn the cakes over and air-fry for another 5 minutes. Serve the crab cakes with tartar sauce or cocktail sauce, or dress it up with the suggestion below.

Variations & Ingredients Tips:

> Add some Old Bay seasoning or Cajun spice to the mix.
> Form into mini crab cakes and serve as an appetizer.
> Top with a lemon-herb aioli or spicy remoulade.

Per Serving: Calories: 420; Total Fat: 24g; Saturated Fat: 5g; Cholesterol: 275mg; Sodium: 1720mg; Total Carbs: 21g; Dietary Fiber: 1g; Total Sugars: 3g; Protein: 32g

Mediterranean Salmon Cakes

Servings: 4 | Prep Time: 15 Minutes | Cooking Time: 30 Minutes

Ingredients:

- 1/4 cup heavy cream
- 5 tbsp mayonnaise
- 2 cloves garlic, minced
- 1/4 tsp caper juice
- 2 tsp lemon juice
- 1 tbsp capers
- 1 can salmon
- 2 tsp lemon zest
- 1 egg
- 1/4 minced red bell peppers
- 1/2 cup flour
- 1/8 tsp salt
- 2 tbsp sliced green olives

Directions:

1. Combine heavy cream, 2 tbsp mayonnaise, garlic, caper juices, capers, and lemon juice in a bowl. Place the resulting caper sauce in the fridge until ready to use.
2. Preheat air fryer to 200°C/400°F.
3. Combine canned salmon, lemon zest, egg, remaining mayonnaise, bell peppers, flour, and salt in a bowl. Form into 8 patties.
4. Place the patties in the greased frying basket and Air Fry for 10 minutes, turning once.
5. Let rest for 5 minutes before drizzling with lemon sauce. Garnish with green olives to serve.

Variations & Ingredients Tips:

> Use fresh salmon instead of canned.
> Add breadcrumbs or panko to the patty mixture to bind.
> Serve on a bed of greens or with roasted veggies.

Per Serving: Calories: 375, Total Fat: 27g, Saturated Fat: 6g, Cholesterol: 135mg, Sodium: 530mg, Total Carbs: 16g, Fiber: 1g, Sugars: 2g, Protein: 18g

Cilantro Sea Bass

Servings: 2 | Prep Time: 5 Minutes | Cooking Time: 15 Minutes

Ingredients:

- Salt and pepper to taste
- 1 tsp olive oil
- 2 sea bass fillets
- 1/2 tsp berbere seasoning
- 2 tsp chopped cilantro
- 1 tsp dried thyme
- 1/2 tsp garlic powder
- 4 lemon quarters

Directions:

1. Preheat air fryer at 190°C/375°F.
2. Rub sea bass fillets with olive oil, thyme, garlic powder, salt and black pepper. Season with berbere seasoning.
3. Place fillets in the greased frying basket and Air Fry for 6-8 minutes. Let rest for 5 minutes on a serving plate.
4. Scatter with cilantro and serve with lemon quarters on the side.

Variations & Ingredients Tips:

- Use cod, halibut or snapper instead of sea bass.
- Add a sprinkle of smoked paprika or cayenne for heat.
- Serve over a bed of cilantro-lime rice or quinoa.

Per Serving: Calories: 220; Total Fat: 8g; Saturated Fat: 1.5g; Cholesterol: 70mg; Sodium: 200mg; Total Carbs: 2g; Dietary Fiber: 1g; Total Sugars: 0g; Protein: 34g

Vegetarian Recipes

Spinach & Brie Frittata

Servings: 4 | Prep Time: 10 Minutes | Cooking Time: 25 Minutes

Ingredients:

- 5 eggs
- Salt and pepper to taste
- ½ cup baby spinach
- 1 shallot, diced
- 113 grams brie cheese, cubed
- 1 tomato, sliced

Directions:

1. Preheat air fryer to 160°C/320°F.
2. Whisk all ingredients, except for the tomato slices, in a bowl.
3. Transfer to a baking pan greased with olive oil and top with tomato slices.
4. Place the pan in the air fryer basket and Bake for 14 minutes.
5. Let cool for 5 minutes before slicing. Serve and enjoy!

Variations & Ingredients Tips:

- Substitute brie with goat cheese, feta, or cheddar.
- Add sliced mushrooms, bell peppers, or zucchini to the mix.
- Top with sliced avocado or a dollop of sour cream.

Per Serving: Calories: 220; Total Fat: 16g; Saturated Fat: 8g; Sodium: 320mg; Total Carbohydrates: 3g; Dietary Fiber: 0g; Total Sugars: 2g; Protein: 15g

Tomato & Squash Stuffed Mushrooms

Servings: 2 | Prep Time: 10 Minutes | Cooking Time: 15 Minutes

Ingredients:

- 12 whole white button mushrooms
- 3 tsp olive oil
- 2 tbsp diced zucchini
- 1 tsp soy sauce
- ¼ tsp salt
- 2 tbsp tomato paste
- 1 tbsp chopped parsley

Directions:

1. Preheat air fryer to 180°C/350°F.
2. Remove the stems from the mushrooms. Chop the stems finely and set in a bowl. Brush 1 tsp of olive oil around the top ridge of mushroom caps.
3. To the bowl of the stem, add all ingredients, except for parsley, and mix.
4. Divide and press mixture into tops of mushroom caps.
5. Place the mushrooms in the air fryer basket and Air Fry for 5 minutes.
6. Top with parsley. Serve.

Variations & Ingredients Tips:

- Use portobello mushrooms instead of button mushrooms for a larger appetizer.
- Substitute zucchini with eggplant, yellow squash, or bell peppers.
- Add grated Parmesan cheese or bread crumbs to the filling for extra flavor and texture.

Per Serving: Calories: 130; Total Fat: 10g; Saturated Fat: 1.5g; Sodium: 490mg; Total Carbohydrates: 7g; Dietary Fiber: 2g; Total Sugars: 4g; Protein: 4g

Basic Fried Tofu

Servings: 4 | Prep Time: 10 Minutes (plus 1 Hour Marinating Time) | Cooking Time: 17 Minutes

Ingredients:

- 400 grams extra-firm tofu, drained and pressed
- 1 tablespoon sesame oil
- 2 tablespoons low-sodium soy sauce
- ¼ cup rice vinegar
- 1 tablespoon fresh grated ginger
- 1 clove garlic, minced
- 3 tablespoons cornstarch
- ¼ teaspoon black pepper
- ⅛ teaspoon salt

Directions:

1. Cut the tofu into 16 cubes. Set aside in a glass container with a lid.
2. In a medium bowl, mix the sesame oil, soy sauce, rice vinegar, ginger, and garlic. Pour over the tofu and secure the lid. Place in the refrigerator to marinate for an hour.
3. Preheat the air fryer to 175°C/350°F.
4. In a small bowl, mix the cornstarch, black pepper, and salt.
5. Transfer the tofu to a large bowl and discard the leftover marinade. Pour the cornstarch mixture over the tofu and toss until all the pieces are coated.
6. Liberally spray the air fryer basket with olive oil mist and set the tofu pieces inside. Allow space between the tofu so it can cook evenly. Cook in batches if necessary.
7. Cook 15 to 17 minutes, shaking the basket every 5 minutes to allow the tofu to cook evenly on all sides. When it's done cooking, the tofu will be crisped and browned on all sides.
8. Remove the tofu from the air fryer basket and serve warm.

Variations & Ingredients Tips:

- Add a dash of sriracha or red pepper flakes to the marinade for a spicy kick.
- Serve the fried tofu with a dipping sauce like sweet chili sauce or peanut sauce.
- Use the fried tofu in stir-fries, salads, or rice bowls for a protein-packed meal.

Per Serving: Calories: 180; Cholesterol: 0mg; Total Fat: 11g; Saturated Fat: 1g; Sodium: 370mg; Total Carbohydrates: 10g; Dietary Fiber: 1g; Total Sugars: 1g; Protein: 11g

Quinoa Burgers With Feta Cheese And Dill

Servings: 6 | Prep Time: 30 Minutes | Cooking Time: 10 Minutes

Ingredients:

- 1 cup quinoa (red, white or multi-colored)
- 1½ cups water
- 1 teaspoon salt
- freshly ground black pepper
- 1½ cups rolled oats
- 3 eggs, lightly beaten
- ¼ cup minced white onion
- ½ cup crumbled feta cheese
- ¼ cup chopped fresh dill
- salt and freshly ground black pepper
- vegetable or canola oil, in a spray bottle
- whole-wheat hamburger buns (or gluten-free hamburger buns*)
- arugula
- tomato, sliced
- red onion, sliced
- mayonnaise

Directions:

1. Make the quinoa: Rinse the quinoa in cold water in

a saucepan, swirling it with your hand until any dry husks rise to the surface. Drain the quinoa as well as you can and then put the saucepan on the stovetop to dry and toast the quinoa. Turn the heat to medium-high and shake the pan regularly until you see the quinoa moving easily and can hear the seeds moving in the pan, indicating that they are dry. Add the water, salt and pepper. Bring the liquid to a boil and then reduce the heat to low or medium-low. You should see just a few bubbles, not a boil. Cover with a lid, leaving it askew and simmer for 20 minutes. Turn the heat off and fluff the quinoa with a fork. If there's any liquid left in the bottom of the pot, place it back on the burner for another 3 minutes or so. Spread the cooked quinoa out on a sheet pan to cool.

2. Combine the room temperature quinoa in a large bowl with the oats, eggs, onion, cheese and dill. Season with salt and pepper and mix well (remember that feta cheese is salty). Shape the mixture into 6 patties with flat sides (so they fit more easily into the air fryer). Add a little water or a few more rolled oats if necessary to get the mixture to be the right consistency to make patties.
3. Preheat the air-fryer to 200°C/400°F.
4. Spray both sides of the patties generously with oil and transfer them to the air fryer basket in one layer (you will probably have to cook these burgers in batches, depending on the size of your air fryer). Air-fry each batch at 200°C/400°F for 10 minutes, flipping the burgers over halfway through the cooking time.
5. Build your burger on the whole-wheat hamburger buns with arugula, tomato, red onion and mayonnaise.

Variations & Ingredients Tips:

- Use leftover cooked quinoa to save time. You'll need about 2½ cups cooked.
- Substitute feta with goat cheese or shredded cheddar.
- Add grated carrots or zucchini for extra veggies and moisture.

Per Serving: Calories: 370; Total Fat: 15g; Saturated Fat: 5g; Sodium: 650mg; Total Carbohydrates: 46g; Dietary Fiber: 7g; Total Sugars: 4g; Protein: 16g

Roasted Vegetable Stromboli

Servings: 2 | Prep Time: 30 Minutes | Cooking Time: 29 Minutes

Ingredients:

- ½ onion, thinly sliced
- ½ red pepper, julienned
- ½ yellow pepper, julienned
- olive oil
- 1 small zucchini, thinly sliced
- 1 cup thinly sliced mushrooms
- 1½ cups chopped broccoli
- 1 teaspoon Italian seasoning
- salt and freshly ground black pepper
- ½ recipe of Blue Jean Chef Pizza dough (page 231) OR 1 (400-gram) tube refrigerated pizza dough
- 2 cups grated mozzarella cheese
- ¼ cup grated Parmesan cheese
- ½ cup sliced black olives, optional
- dried oregano
- pizza or marinara sauce

Directions:

1. Preheat the air fryer to 200°C/400°F.
2. Toss the onions and peppers with a little olive oil and air-fry the vegetables for 7 minutes, shaking the basket once or twice while the vegetables cook.
3. Add the zucchini, mushrooms, broccoli and Italian seasoning to the basket. Add a little more olive oil and season with salt and freshly ground black pepper. Air-fry for an additional 7 minutes, shaking the basket halfway through. Let the vegetables cool slightly while you roll out the pizza dough.
4. On a lightly floured surface, roll or press the pizza dough out into a 33-cm by 28-cm rectangle, with the long side closest to you. Sprinkle half of the mozzarella and Parmesan cheeses over the dough leaving an empty 2.5-cm border from the edge farthest away from you. Spoon the roasted vegetables over the cheese, sprinkle the olives over everything and top with the remaining cheese.
5. Start rolling the stromboli away from you and toward the empty border. Make sure the filling stays tightly tucked inside the roll. Finally, tuck the ends of the dough in and pinch the seam shut. Place the seam side down and shape the stromboli into a U-shape to fit into the air fryer basket. Cut 4 small slits with the tip of a sharp knife evenly in the top of the dough, lightly brush the stromboli with a little oil and sprinkle with some dried oregano.
6. Preheat the air fryer to 180°C/360°F.
7. Spray or brush the air fryer basket with oil and transfer the U-shaped stromboli to the air fryer basket. Air-fry for 15 minutes, flipping the stromboli over after the first 10 minutes. (Use a plate to invert the Stromboli out of the air fryer basket and then slide it back into the basket off the plate.)
8. To remove, carefully flip the stromboli over onto a cutting board. Let it rest for a couple of minutes before serving. Cut it into 5-cm slices and serve with pizza or marinara sauce.

Variations & Ingredients Tips:

- Use store-bought pizza dough for a quicker prep.
- Add sun-dried tomatoes, artichoke hearts, or roasted garlic for extra flavor.
- Brush the dough with pesto before adding the fillings.

Per Serving: Calories: 820; Total Fat: 41g; Saturated Fat: 18g; Sodium: 1580mg; Total Carbohydrates: 81g; Dietary Fiber: 8g; Total Sugars: 10g; Protein: 38g

Vegetarian Paella

Servings: 3 | Prep Time: 10 Minutes | Cooking Time: 50 Minutes

Ingredients:

- 1/2 cup chopped artichoke hearts
- 1/2 sliced red bell peppers
- 4 mushrooms, thinly sliced
- 1/2 cup canned diced tomatoes
- 1/2 cup canned chickpeas
- 3 tbsp hot sauce
- 2 tbsp lemon juice
- 1 tbsp allspice
- 1 cup rice

Directions:

1. Preheat air fryer to 200°C/400°F.
2. Combine the artichokes, peppers, mushrooms, tomatoes and their juices, chickpeas, hot sauce, lemon juice, and allspice in a baking pan.
3. Roast for 10 minutes.
4. Pour in rice and 2 cups of boiling water, cover with aluminum foil, and Roast for 22 minutes.
5. Discard the foil and Roast for 3 minutes until the top is crisp.
6. Let cool slightly before stirring. Serve.

Variations & Ingredients Tips:

- Use vegetable or mushroom broth instead of water.
- Add sliced vegan sausages or chickpea "shrimp".
- Garnish with lemon wedges and fresh parsley.

Per Serving: Calories: 320; Total Fat: 3g; Saturated Fat: 0g; Sodium: 768mg; Total Carbohydrates: 67g; Dietary Fiber: 8g; Total Sugars: 7g; Protein: 9g

Spinach And Cheese Calzone

Servings: 2 | Prep Time: 20 Minutes | Cooking Time: 10 Minutes

Ingredients:

- ⅔ cup frozen chopped spinach, thawed
- 1 cup grated mozzarella cheese
- 1 cup ricotta cheese
- ½ teaspoon Italian seasoning
- ½ teaspoon salt
- freshly ground black pepper
- 1 store-bought or homemade pizza dough* (about 340 to 454 grams)
- 2 tablespoons olive oil
- pizza or marinara sauce (optional)

Directions:

1. Drain and squeeze all the water out of the thawed spinach and set it aside. Mix the mozzarella cheese, ricotta cheese, Italian seasoning, salt and freshly ground black pepper together in a bowl. Stir in the chopped spinach.
2. Divide the dough in half. With floured hands or on a floured surface, stretch or roll one half of the dough into a 25-cm circle. Spread half of the cheese and spinach mixture on half of the dough, leaving about 5 cm of dough empty around the edge.
3. Fold the other half of the dough over the cheese mixture, almost to the edge of the bottom dough to form a half moon. Fold the bottom edge of dough up over the top edge and crimp the dough around the edges in order to make the crust and seal the calzone. Brush the dough with olive oil. Repeat with the second half of dough to make the second calzone.
4. Preheat the air fryer to 180°C/360°F.
5. Brush or spray the air fryer basket with olive oil. Air-fry the calzones one at a time for 10 minutes, flipping the calzone over half way through. Serve with warm pizza or marinara sauce if desired.

Variations & Ingredients Tips:

- Add sautéed mushrooms, onions, or bell peppers to the filling.
- Use a combination of different cheeses like feta, provolone, or Parmesan.
- Brush the calzone with garlic butter or sprinkle with Italian seasoning before air frying.

Per Serving: Calories: 790; Total Fat: 41g; Saturated Fat: 19g; Sodium: 1480mg; Total Carbohydrates: 70g; Dietary Fiber: 4g; Total Sugars: 4g; Protein: 38g

Harissa Veggie Fries

Servings: 4 | Prep Time: 20 Minutes | Cooking Time: 55 Minutes

Ingredients:

- 454 grams red potatoes, cut into rounds
- 1 onion, diced
- 1 green bell pepper, diced
- 1 red bell pepper, diced
- 2 tbsp olive oil
- Salt and pepper to taste
- ¾ tsp garlic powder
- ¾ tsp harissa seasoning

Directions:

1. Combine all ingredients in a large bowl and mix until potatoes are well coated and seasoned.
2. Preheat air fryer to 180°C/350°F.
3. Pour all of the contents in the bowl into the air fryer basket.
4. Bake for 35 minutes, shaking every 10 minutes, until golden brown and soft.
5. Serve hot.

Variations & Ingredients Tips:

- Substitute red potatoes with sweet potatoes or yams for a sweeter flavor.
- Add other vegetables like carrots, zucchini, or eggplant for variety.
- Adjust the amount of harissa seasoning to make the fries spicier or milder.

Per Serving: Calories: 200; Total Fat: 7g; Saturated Fat: 1g; Sodium: 135mg; Total Carbohydrates: 31g; Dietary Fiber: 4g; Total Sugars: 5g; Protein: 4g

Sesame Orange Tofu With Snow Peas

Servings: 4 | Prep Time: 20 Minutes | Cooking Time: 40 Minutes

Ingredients:

- 400 grams tofu, cubed
- 1 tbsp tamari
- 1 tsp olive oil
- 1 tsp sesame oil
- 1 ½ tbsp cornstarch, divided
- ½ tsp salt
- ¼ tsp garlic powder
- 1 cup snow peas
- ½ cup orange juice
- ¼ cup vegetable broth
- 1 orange, zested
- 1 garlic clove, minced
- ¼ tsp ground ginger
- 2 scallions, chopped
- 1 tbsp sesame seeds
- 2 cups cooked jasmine rice
- 2 tbsp chopped parsley

Directions:

1. Preheat air fryer to 200°C/400°F.
2. Combine tofu, tamari, olive oil, and sesame oil in a large bowl until tofu is coated. Add in 1 tablespoon cornstarch, salt, and garlic powder and toss.
3. Arrange the tofu on the air fryer basket. Air Fry for 5 minutes, then shake the basket. Add snow peas and Air Fry for 5 minutes. Place tofu mixture in a bowl.
4. Bring the orange juice, vegetable broth, orange zest, garlic, and ginger to a boil over medium heat in a small saucepan. Whisk the rest of the cornstarch and 1 tablespoon water in a small bowl to make a slurry. Pour the slurry into the saucepan and constantly stir for 2 minutes until the sauce has thickened. Let off the heat for 2 minutes.
5. Pour the orange sauce, scallions, and sesame seeds in the bowl with the tofu and stir to coat.
6. Serve with jasmine rice sprinkled with parsley. Enjoy!

Variations & Ingredients Tips:

- Use tempeh or seitan instead of tofu for a different texture.
- Add sliced bell peppers, mushrooms, or carrots to the stir-fry.
- Serve over quinoa, brown rice, or rice noodles for variation.

Per Serving: Calories: 360; Total Fat: 14g; Saturated Fat: 2g; Sodium: 610mg; Total Carbohydrates: 45g; Dietary Fiber: 4g; Total Sugars: 8g; Protein: 16g

Quinoa & Black Bean Stuffed Peppers

Servings: 4 | Prep Time: 15 Minutes | Cooking Time: 30 Minutes

Ingredients:

- ½ cup vegetable broth
- ½ cup quinoa
- 1 can black beans
- ½ cup diced red onion
- 1 garlic clove, minced
- ½ tsp salt
- ½ tsp ground cumin
- ¼ tsp paprika
- ¼ tsp ancho chili powder

- 4 bell peppers, any color
- ½ cup grated cheddar
- ¼ cup chopped cilantro
- ½ cup red enchilada sauce

Directions:

1. Add vegetable broth and quinoa to a small saucepan over medium heat. Bring to a boil, then cover and let it simmer for 5 minutes. Turn off the heat.
2. Preheat air fryer to 180°C/350°F.
3. Transfer quinoa to a medium bowl and stir in black beans, onion, red enchilada sauce, ancho chili powder, garlic, salt, cumin, and paprika.
4. Cut the top 0.5-cm off the bell peppers. Remove seeds and membranes. Scoop quinoa filling into each pepper and top with cheddar cheese.
5. Transfer peppers to the air fryer basket and bake for 10 minutes until peppers are soft and filling is heated through.
6. Garnish with cilantro. Serve warm along with salsa. Enjoy!

Variations & Ingredients Tips:

- Use any color quinoa - white, red, or tricolor.
- Substitute black beans with pinto or kidney beans.
- Add cooked ground beef or turkey for a non-vegetarian version.

Per Serving: Calories: 320; Total Fat: 10g; Saturated Fat: 5g; Sodium: 890mg; Total Carbohydrates: 46g; Dietary Fiber: 12g; Total Sugars: 8g; Protein: 16g

Vegetarian Eggplant "pizzas"

Servings: 4 | Prep Time: 15 Minutes | Cooking Time: 25 Minutes

Ingredients:

- 1/2 cup diced baby bella mushrooms
- 3 tbsp olive oil
- 1/4 cup diced onions
- 1/2 cup pizza sauce
- 1 eggplant, sliced
- 1 tsp salt
- 1 cup shredded mozzarella
- 1/4 cup chopped oregano

Directions:

1. Warm 2 tsp of olive oil in a skillet over medium heat. Add in onion and mushrooms and stir-fry for 4 minutes until tender.
2. Stir in pizza sauce. Turn the heat off.
3. Preheat air fryer to 190°C/375°F.
4. Brush the eggplant slices with the remaining olive oil on both sides. Lay out slices on a large plate and season with salt.
5. Top with the sauce mixture and shredded mozzarella.
6. Place the eggplant pizzas in the frying basket and Air Fry for 5 minutes.
7. Garnish with oregano to serve.

Variations & Ingredients Tips:

- Use vegan cheese shreds for a dairy-free version.
- Add sliced olives, bell peppers or other toppings.
- Brush with garlic olive oil for extra flavor.

Per Serving: Calories: 217; Total Fat: 14g; Saturated Fat: 4g; Sodium: 693mg; Total Carbohydrates: 18g; Dietary Fiber: 5g; Total Sugars: 8g; Protein: 7g

Easy Zucchini Lasagna Roll-ups

Servings: 2 | Prep Time: 20 Minutes | Cooking Time: 40 Minutes

Ingredients:

- 2 medium zucchini
- 2 tbsp lemon juice
- 1 ½ cups ricotta cheese
- 1 tbsp allspice
- 2 cups marinara sauce
- 1/3 cup mozzarella cheese

Directions:

1. Preheat air fryer to 200°C/400°F. Cut the ends of each zucchini, then slice into 6-mm thick pieces and drizzle with lemon juice. Roast for 5 minutes until slightly tender. Let cool slightly. Combine ricotta cheese and allspice in a bowl; set aside. Spread 2 tbsp of marinara sauce on the bottom of a baking pan. Spoon 1-2 tbsp of the ricotta mixture onto each slice, roll up each slice and place them spiral-side up in the pan. Scatter with the remaining ricotta mixture and drizzle with marinara sauce. Top with mozzarella cheese and Bake at 180°C/360°F for 20 minutes until the cheese is bubbly and golden brown. Serve warm.

Variations & Ingredients Tips:

- Substitute zucchini with eggplant or lasagna noodles for different textures.
- Add minced garlic, basil, or oregano to the ricotta mixture for extra flavor.
- Top with grated Parmesan cheese or breadcrumbs before baking for a crispy crust.

Per Serving: Calories: 470; Cholesterol: 80mg; Total Fat: 25g; Saturated Fat: 15g; Sodium: 1060mg; Total Carbohydrates: 38g; Dietary Fiber: 7g; Total Sugars: 22g; Protein: 29g

Tandoori Paneer Naan Pizza

Servings: 4 | Prep Time: 15 Minutes | Cooking Time: 10 Minutes

Ingredients:

- 6 tablespoons plain Greek yogurt, divided
- 1 1/4 teaspoons garam masala, divided
- 1/2 teaspoon turmeric, divided
- 1/4 teaspoon garlic powder
- 1/2 teaspoon paprika, divided
- 1/2 teaspoon black pepper, divided
- 85g paneer, cut into small cubes
- 1 tablespoon extra-virgin olive oil
- 2 teaspoons minced garlic
- 4 cups baby spinach
- 2 tablespoons marinara sauce
- 1/4 teaspoon salt
- 2 plain naan breads (approximately 15cm in diameter)
- 1/2 cup shredded part-skim mozzarella cheese

Directions:

1. Preheat air fryer to 180°C/350°F.
2. Marinate paneer in 2 tbsp yogurt, 1/2 tsp garam masala, 1/4 tsp turmeric, garlic powder, 1/4 tsp paprika, 1/4 tsp pepper for 1 hour.
3. Sauté garlic in olive oil, then add spinach and remaining yogurt, marinara, spices and salt.
4. Divide spinach mixture between naans, top with marinated paneer.
5. Air fry one naan at a time for 4 mins. Top with 1/4 cup mozzarella and cook 4 more mins.
6. Repeat with second naan. Serve warm.

Variations & Ingredients Tips:

- Use naan alternatives like pita or tortilla for the base.
- Add sautéed onions, bell peppers or mushrooms to the topping.
- Brush naans with garlic butter before baking.

Per Serving: Calories: 252; Total Fat: 11g; Saturated Fat: 4g; Sodium: 592mg; Total Carbohydrates: 28g; Dietary Fiber: 3g; Total Sugars: 5g; Protein: 12g

Pinto Taquitos

Servings: 4 | Prep Time: 20 Minutes | Cooking Time: 8 Minutes

Ingredients:

- 12 corn tortillas (15- to 18-cm size)
- Filling
- 1/2 cup refried pinto beans
- 1/2 cup grated sharp Cheddar or Pepper Jack cheese
- 1/4 cup corn kernels (if frozen, measure after thawing and draining)
- 2 tablespoons chopped green onion
- 2 tablespoons chopped jalapeño pepper (seeds and ribs removed before chopping)
- 1/2 teaspoon lime juice
- 1/2 teaspoon chile powder, plus extra for dusting
- 1/2 teaspoon cumin
- 1/2 teaspoon garlic powder
- oil for misting or cooking spray
- salsa, sour cream, or guacamole for dipping

Directions:

1. Mix together all filling Ingredients.
2. Warm refrigerated tortillas for easier rolling. (Wrap in damp paper towels and microwave for 30 to 60 seconds.)
3. Working with one at a time, place 1 tablespoon of filling on tortilla and roll up. Spray with oil or cooking spray and dust outside with chile powder to taste.
4. Place 6 taquitos in air fryer basket (4 on bottom layer, 2 stacked crosswise on top). Cook at 200°C/390°F for 8 minutes, until crispy and brown.
5. Repeat step 4 to cook remaining taquitos.
6. Serve plain or with salsa, sour cream, or guacamole for dipping.

Variations & Ingredients Tips:

- Use black beans or kidney beans instead of pinto beans.
- Add cooked shredded chicken or ground beef for a non-vegetarian version.
- Serve with shredded lettuce, diced tomatoes, and sliced avocado.

Per Serving: Calories: 280; Total Fat: 11g; Saturated Fat: 4.5g; Sodium: 520mg; Total Carbohydrates: 37g; Dietary Fiber: 6g; Total Sugars: 2g; Protein: 11g

Rainbow Quinoa Patties

Servings: 4 | Prep Time: 10 Minutes | Cooking Time: 20 Minutes

Ingredients:

- 1 cup canned tri-bean blend, drained and rinsed
- 2 tbsp olive oil
- ½ tsp ground cumin
- ½ tsp garlic salt
- 1 tbsp paprika
- 1/3 cup uncooked quinoa
- 2 tbsp chopped onion
- ¼ cup shredded carrot
- 2 tbsp chopped cilantro
- 1 tsp chili powder
- ½ tsp salt
- 2 tbsp mascarpone cheese

Directions:

1. Place 1/3 cup of water, 1 tbsp of olive oil, cumin, and salt in a saucepan over medium heat and bring it to a boil. Remove from the heat and stir in quinoa. Let rest covered for 5 minutes.
2. Preheat air fryer at 180°C/350°F.
3. Using the back of a fork, mash beans until smooth. Toss in cooked quinoa and the remaining ingredients.
4. Form mixture into 4 patties. Place patties in the greased air fryer basket and Air Fry for 6 minutes, turning once, and brush with the remaining olive oil.
5. Serve immediately.

Variations & Ingredients Tips:

- Use any combination of canned beans like black beans, kidney beans, or chickpeas.
- Add grated zucchini or sweet potato for extra moisture and nutrients.
- Serve with yogurt dip or guacamole.

Per Serving: Calories: 240; Total Fat: 12g; Saturated Fat: 3g; Sodium: 660mg; Total Carbohydrates: 26g; Dietary Fiber: 6g; Total Sugars: 2g; Protein: 8g

Zucchini Tamale Pie

Servings: 4 | Prep Time: 15 Minutes | Cooking Time: 45 Minutes

Ingredients:

- 1 cup canned diced tomatoes with juice
- 1 zucchini, diced
- 3 tbsp safflower oil
- 1 cup cooked pinto beans
- 3 garlic cloves, minced
- 1 tbsp corn masa flour
- 1 tsp dried oregano
- 1/2 tsp ground cumin
- 1 tsp onion powder
- Salt to taste
- 1/2 tsp red chili flakes
- 1/2 cup ground cornmeal
- 1 tsp nutritional yeast
- 2 tbsp chopped cilantro
- 1/2 tsp lime zest

Directions:

1. Warm 2 tbsp of the oil in a skillet over medium heat and sauté the zucchini for 3 minutes or until they begin to brown.
2. Add the beans, tomatoes, garlic, flour, oregano, cumin, onion powder, salt, and chili flakes. Cook for 5 minutes until thick.
3. Remove from heat. Spray a baking pan with oil and pour the mix inside. Smooth the top and set aside.
4. In a pot, add the cornmeal, 1 1/2 cups water, and salt. Whisk as it boils. Reduce heat to low.
5. Add the yeast and oil and cook for 10 minutes, stirring often, until thick.
6. Remove. Preheat air fryer to 165°C/325°F.
7. Add cilantro and lime zest into the cornmeal mix and combine.
8. Spread it over the filling to form a crust topping.
9. Put in the frying basket and Bake for 20 minutes until golden.
10. Let cool for 5-10 minutes, then cut and serve.

Variations & Ingredients Tips:

- Use gluten-free cornmeal or masa harina for crust.
- Add vegan cheese shreds to the filling.
- Top with avocado slices and salsa.

Per Serving: Calories: 328; Total Fat: 15g; Saturated Fat: 1g; Sodium: 290mg; Total Carbohydrates: 45g; Dietary Fiber: 9g; Total Sugars: 7g; Protein: 9g

Tex-mex Potatoes With Avocado Dressing

Servings: 2 | Prep Time: 20 Minutes | Cooking Time: 60 Minutes

Ingredients:

- ¼ cup chopped parsley, dill, cilantro, chives
- ¼ cup yogurt
- ½ avocado, diced
- 2 tbsp milk
- 2 tsp lemon juice
- ½ tsp lemon zest
- 1 green onion, chopped
- 2 cloves garlic, quartered
- Salt and pepper to taste
- 2 tsp olive oil
- 2 russet potatoes, scrubbed and perforated with a fork
- 1 cup steamed broccoli florets
- ½ cup canned white beans

Directions:

1. In a food processor, blend the yogurt, avocado, milk, lemon juice, lemon zest, green onion, garlic, parsley, dill, cilantro, chives, salt and pepper until smooth. Transfer it to a small bowl and let chill the dressing covered in the fridge until ready to use.
2. Preheat air fryer at 200°C/400°F. Rub olive oil over both potatoes and sprinkle with salt and pepper. Place them in the air fryer basket and Bake for 45 minutes, flipping at 30 minutes mark.
3. Let cool onto a cutting board for 5 minutes until cool enough to handle. Cut each potato lengthwise into slices and pinch ends together to open up each slice.
4. Stuff broccoli and beans into potatoes and put them back into the basket, and cook for 3 more minutes.
5. Drizzle avocado dressing over and serve.

Variations & Ingredients Tips:

- Substitute russet potatoes with sweet potatoes or yams.
- Use cauliflower florets or asparagus instead of broccoli.
- Add cooked quinoa or brown rice to the stuffing.

Per Serving: Calories: 450; Total Fat: 18g; Saturated Fat: 3g; Sodium: 250mg; Total Carbohydrates: 64g; Dietary Fiber: 12g; Total Sugars: 5g; Protein: 14g

Veggie Fried Rice

Servings: 4 | Prep Time: 10 Minutes | Cooking Time: 25 Minutes

Ingredients:

- 1 cup cooked brown rice
- 1/3 cup chopped onion
- 1/2 cup chopped carrots
- 1/2 cup chopped bell peppers
- 1/2 cup chopped broccoli florets
- 3 tablespoons low-sodium soy sauce
- 1 tablespoon sesame oil
- 1 teaspoon ground ginger
- 1 teaspoon ground garlic powder
- 1/2 teaspoon black pepper
- 1/8 teaspoon salt
- 2 large eggs

Directions:

1. Preheat the air fryer to 190°C/370°F.
2. In a large bowl, mix together the brown rice, onions, carrots, bell pepper, and broccoli.
3. In a small bowl, whisk together the soy sauce, sesame oil, ginger, garlic powder, pepper, salt, and eggs.
4. Pour the egg mixture into the rice and vegetable mixture and mix together.
5. Liberally spray a 18-cm springform pan (or compatible air fryer dish) with olive oil. Add the rice mixture to the pan and cover with aluminum foil.
6. Place a metal trivet into the air fryer basket and set the pan on top. Cook for 15 minutes.
7. Carefully remove the pan from basket, discard the foil, and mix the rice. Return the rice to the air fryer basket, turning down the temperature to 180°C/350°F and cooking another 10 minutes.
8. Remove and let cool 5 minutes. Serve warm.

Variations & Ingredients Tips:

- Add diced tofu or edamame for extra protein.
- Use cauliflower rice for a low-carb option.
- Drizzle with sriracha or chili garlic sauce for heat.

Per Serving: Calories: 253; Total Fat: 8g; Saturated Fat: 1g; Sodium: 553mg; Total Carbohydrates: 38g; Dietary Fiber: 5g; Total Sugars: 5g; Protein: 8g

Spicy Sesame Tempeh Slaw With Peanut Dressing

Servings: 2 | Prep Time: 20 Minutes (plus Marinating Time) | Cooking Time: 8 Minutes

Ingredients:

- 2 cups hot water
- 1 teaspoon salt
- 227 grams tempeh, sliced into 2.5-cm-long pieces
- 2 tablespoons low-sodium soy sauce
- 2 tablespoons rice vinegar
- 1 tablespoon filtered water

- 2 teaspoons sesame oil
- ½ teaspoon fresh ginger
- 1 clove garlic, minced
- ¼ teaspoon black pepper
- ½ jalapeño, sliced
- 4 cups cabbage slaw
- 4 tablespoons Peanut Dressing (see the following recipe)
- 2 tablespoons fresh chopped cilantro
- 2 tablespoons chopped peanuts

Directions:

1. Mix the hot water with the salt and pour over the tempeh in a glass bowl. Stir and cover with a towel for 10 minutes.
2. Discard the water and leave the tempeh in the bowl.
3. In a medium bowl, mix the soy sauce, rice vinegar, filtered water, sesame oil, ginger, garlic, pepper, and jalapeño. Pour over the tempeh and cover with a towel. Place in the refrigerator to marinate for at least 2 hours.
4. Preheat the air fryer to 190°C/370°F. Remove the tempeh from the bowl and discard the remaining marinade.
5. Liberally spray the metal trivet that goes into the air fryer basket and place the tempeh on top of the trivet.
6. Cook for 4 minutes, flip, and cook another 4 minutes.
7. In a large bowl, mix the cabbage slaw with the Peanut Dressing and toss in the cilantro and chopped peanuts.
8. Portion onto 4 plates and place the cooked tempeh on top when cooking completes. Serve immediately.

Variations & Ingredients Tips:

- Use extra-firm tofu instead of tempeh for a different protein.
- Add shredded carrots, bell peppers, or edamame to the slaw.
- Substitute peanut dressing with a sesame-ginger dressing.

Per Serving: Calories: 380; Total Fat: 23g; Saturated Fat: 3.5g; Sodium: 1210mg; Total Carbohydrates: 29g; Dietary Fiber: 8g; Total Sugars: 8g; Protein: 22g

Berbere Eggplant Dip

Servings: 4 | Prep Time: 10 Minutes | Cooking Time: 35 Minutes

Ingredients:

- 1 eggplant, halved lengthwise
- 3 tsp olive oil
- 2 tsp pine nuts
- ¼ cup tahini
- 1 tbsp lemon juice
- 2 cloves garlic, minced
- ¼ tsp berbere seasoning
- ⅛ tsp ground cumin
- Salt and pepper to taste
- 1 tbsp chopped parsley

Directions:

1. Preheat air fryer to 190°C/370°F. Brush the eggplant with some olive oil. With a fork, pierce the eggplant flesh a few times. Place them, flat sides-down, in the frying basket. Air Fry for 25 minutes. Transfer the eggplant to a cutting board and let cool for 3 minutes until easy to handle. Place pine nuts in the frying basket and Air Fry for 2 minutes, shaking every 30 seconds. Set aside in a bowl.
2. Scoop out the eggplant flesh and add to a food processor. Add in tahini, lemon juice, garlic, berbere seasoning, cumin, salt, and black pepper and pulse until smooth. Transfer to a serving bowl. Scatter with toasted pine nuts, parsley, and the remaining olive oil. Serve immediately.

Variations & Ingredients Tips:

- Substitute berbere seasoning with harissa or ras el hanout for a different spice profile.
- Serve with pita chips, crudités, or crackers for dipping.
- Add roasted red peppers or sun-dried tomatoes to the dip for extra flavor and color.

Per Serving: Calories: 170; Cholesterol: 0mg; Total Fat: 14g; Saturated Fat: 2g; Sodium: 85mg; Total Carbohydrates: 10g; Dietary Fiber: 4g; Total Sugars: 4g; Protein: 5g

Vegetable Side Dishes Recipes

Caraway Seed Pretzel Sticks

Servings: 4 | Prep Time: 10 Minutes | Cooking Time: 30 Minutes

Ingredients:

- ½ pizza dough
- 1 tsp baking soda
- 2 tbsp caraway seeds

Directions:

1. Preheat air fryer to 200°C/400°F.
2. Roll out the dough, on parchment paper, into a rectangle, then cut it into 8 strips.
3. Whisk the baking soda and 1 cup of hot water until well dissolved in a bowl. Submerge each strip, shake off any excess, and stretch another 2.5-5cm.
4. Scatter with caraway seeds and let rise for 10 minutes in the frying basket.
5. Grease with cooking spray and Air Fry for 8 minutes until golden brown, turning once.
6. Serve.

Variations & Ingredients Tips:

- Use store-bought pizza dough or make your own from scratch.
- Add grated parmesan or coarse salt to the topping.
- Serve with mustard or beer cheese dip.

Per Serving: Calories: 120; Total Fat: 2g; Saturated Fat: 0g; Cholesterol: 0mg; Sodium: 200mg; Total Carbs: 22g; Fiber: 1g; Sugars: 1g; Protein: 3g

Smoked Avocado Wedges

Servings: 4 | Prep Time: 5 Minutes | Cooking Time: 15 Minutes

Ingredients:

- ½ teaspoon smoked paprika
- 2 teaspoons olive oil
- ½ lime, juiced
- 8 peeled avocado wedges
- 1 teaspoon chipotle powder
- ¼ teaspoon salt

Directions:

1. Preheat air fryer to 200°C/400°F.
2. Drizzle the avocado wedges with olive oil and lime juice.
3. In a bowl, combine chipotle powder, smoked paprika, and salt. Sprinkle over the avocado wedges.
4. Place them in the frying basket and Air Fry for 7 minutes.
5. Serve immediately.

Variations & Ingredients Tips:

- Use lemon juice instead of lime juice for a different citrus flavor.
- Add some chopped cilantro or parsley for a fresh herb flavor.
- Serve the avocado wedges with salsa or guacamole for a Mexican-inspired side dish.

Per Serving: Calories: 130; Total Fat: 12g; Saturated Fat: 1.5g; Cholesterol: 0mg; Sodium: 150mg; Total Carbs: 6g; Fiber: 5g; Sugars: 0g; Protein: 1g

Curried Fruit

Servings: 6 | Prep Time: 10 Minutes | Cooking Time: 20 Minutes

Ingredients:

- 1 cup cubed fresh pineapple
- 1 cup cubed fresh pear (firm, not overly ripe)
- 227g frozen peaches, thawed
- 1 425g can dark, sweet, pitted cherries with juice

- 2 tablespoons brown sugar
- 1 teaspoon curry powder

Directions:

1. Combine all ingredients in a large bowl. Stir gently to mix in the sugar and curry.
2. Pour into air fryer baking pan and cook at 182°C/360°F for 10 minutes.
3. Stir fruit and cook for 10 more minutes.
4. Serve hot.

Variations & Ingredients Tips:

- Add diced mango or papaya for extra tropical flavor.
- Substitute honey or maple syrup for the brown sugar.
- Sprinkle with toasted coconut or chopped nuts before serving.

Per Serving: Calories: 130; Total Fat: 0g; Saturated Fat: 0g; Cholesterol: 0mg; Sodium: 5mg; Total Carbs: 33g; Fiber: 3g; Sugars: 26g; Protein: 1g

Sicilian Arancini

Servings: 4 | Prep Time: 15 Minutes | Cooking Time: 20 Minutes

Ingredients:

- 1/3 minced red bell pepper
- 4 tsp grated Parmesan cheese
- 1 1/4 cups cooked rice
- 1 egg
- 3 tbsp plain flour
- 1/3 cup finely grated carrots
- 2 tbsp minced fresh parsley
- 2 tsp olive oil

Directions:

1. Preheat air fryer to 190°C/380°F.
2. In a bowl, mix together rice, egg, flour, carrots, bell pepper, parsley and Parmesan.
3. Shape mixture into 8 fritter patties.
4. Brush the fritters with olive oil.
5. Place fritters in the air fryer basket in a single layer.
6. Air fry for 8-10 minutes, turning once halfway, until golden brown.
7. Serve hot.

Variations & Ingredients Tips:

- Add finely chopped cooked chicken or ham to the fritter mixture.

- Roll the fritters in breadcrumbs before air frying for extra crunch.
- Serve with a marinara or pesto sauce for dipping.

Per Serving: Calories: 143; Total Fat: 3g; Saturated Fat: 1g; Cholesterol: 47mg; Sodium: 142mg; Total Carbs: 24g; Dietary Fiber: 2g; Total Sugars: 2g; Protein: 5g

Shoestring Butternut Squash Fries

Servings: 3 | Prep Time: 10 Minutes | Cooking Time: 16 Minutes

Ingredients:

- 567g spiralized butternut squash strands
- Vegetable oil spray
- Coarse sea salt or kosher salt to taste

Directions:

1. Preheat air fryer to 190°C/375°F.
2. Place squash strands in a bowl and coat generously with vegetable oil spray, tossing several times to evenly coat.
3. When preheated, spread squash strands in an even layer in the air fryer basket.
4. Air fry for 16 minutes, tossing and rearranging every 4 minutes, until lightly browned and crisp.
5. Transfer squash fries to a bowl and season with salt to taste.
6. Serve hot.

Variations & Ingredients Tips:

- Use sweet potato or beet spirals instead of squash.
- Toss with cajun seasoning, ranch powder or grated parmesan before serving.
- Bake at 204°C/400°F for a crispier fry.

Per Serving: Calories: 92; Total Fat: 1g; Saturated Fat: 0g; Cholesterol: 0mg; Sodium: 75mg; Total Carbs: 20g; Dietary Fiber: 4g; Total Sugars: 4g; Protein: 2g

Truffle Vegetable Croquettes

Servings: 4 | Prep Time: 20 Minutes | Cooking Time: 40 Minutes

Ingredients:

- 2 cooked potatoes, mashed
- 1 cooked carrot, mashed
- 1 tablespoon onion, minced

- 2 eggs, beaten
- 2 tablespoons melted butter
- 1 tablespoon truffle oil
- ½ tablespoon flour
- Salt and pepper to taste

Directions:

1. Preheat air fryer to 180°C/350°F.
2. Sift the flour, salt, and pepper in a bowl and stir to combine.
3. Add the potatoes, carrot, onion, butter, and truffle oil to a separate bowl and mix well.
4. Shape the potato mixture into small bite-sized patties.
5. Dip the potato patties into the beaten eggs, coating thoroughly, then roll in the flour mixture to cover all sides.
6. Arrange the croquettes in the greased frying basket and Air Fry for 14-16 minutes. Halfway through cooking, shake the basket. The croquettes should be crispy and golden.
7. Serve hot and enjoy!

Variations & Ingredients Tips:

- Use different types of vegetables, such as sweet potatoes or parsnips, for a variety of flavors and textures.
- Add some grated Parmesan cheese or nutritional yeast to the potato mixture for a cheesy flavor.
- Serve the croquettes with a dipping sauce, such as garlic aioli or tomato sauce.

Per Serving: Calories: 220; Total Fat: 16g; Saturated Fat: 6g; Cholesterol: 110mg; Sodium: 120mg; Total Carbs: 15g; Fiber: 2g; Sugars: 2g; Protein: 5g

Citrusy Brussels Sprouts

Servings: 4 | Prep Time: 10 Minutes | Cooking Time: 15 Minutes

Ingredients:

- 454g Brussels sprouts, quartered
- 1 clementine, cut into rings
- 2 garlic cloves, minced
- 1 tbsp olive oil
- 1 tbsp butter, melted
- ½ tsp salt

Directions:

1. Preheat air fryer to 182°C/360°F.
2. Add the quartered Brussels sprouts with the garlic, olive oil, butter and salt in a bowl and toss until well coated.
3. Pour the Brussels sprouts into the air fryer, top with the clementine slices.
4. Roast for 10 minutes.
5. Remove from the air fryer and set the clementines aside.
6. Toss the Brussels sprouts and serve.

Variations & Ingredients Tips:

- Use orange or grapefruit sections instead of clementine.
- Add sliced almonds or pecans for crunch.
- Drizzle with balsamic glaze before serving.

Per Serving: Calories: 130; Total Fat: 8g; Saturated Fat: 2g; Cholesterol: 5mg; Sodium: 290mg; Total Carbs: 13g; Fiber: 5g; Sugars: 3g; Protein: 4g

Honey-mustard Asparagus Puffs

Servings: 4 | Prep Time: 10 Minutes | Cooking Time: 35 Minutes

Ingredients:

- 8 asparagus spears
- 1/2 sheet puff pastry
- 2 tbsp honey mustard
- 1 egg, lightly beaten

Directions:

1. Preheat the air fryer to 190°C/375°F.
2. Spread the pastry with honey mustard and cut it into 8 strips.
3. Wrap the pastry, honey mustard-side in, around the asparagus.
4. Put a rack in the frying basket and lay the asparagus spears on the rack.
5. Brush all over pastries with beaten egg and air fry for 12-17 minutes or until the pastry is golden.
6. Serve.

Variations & Ingredients Tips:

- Use puff pastry sheets instead of sheets for easier wrapping.
- Brush with an egg wash before cooking for a shiny finish.
- Sprinkle with parmesan cheese before baking.

Per Serving: Calories: 148; Total Fat: 9g; Saturated Fat: 3g; Cholesterol: 77mg; Sodium: 321mg; Total Carbs: 14g; Dietary Fiber: 1g; Total Sugars: 5g; Protein: 4g

Garlic-parmesan Popcorn

Servings: 2 | Prep Time: 2 Minutes | Cooking Time: 15 Minutes

Ingredients:

- 2 tsp grated Parmesan cheese
- ¼ cup popcorn kernels
- 1 tbsp lemon juice
- 1 tsp garlic powder

Directions:

1. Preheat air fryer to 200°C/400°F. Line basket with foil.
2. Put kernels in a single layer and Grill for 6-8 minutes until popping stops.
3. Remove popped corn to a bowl.
4. Drizzle with lemon juice and toss to coat.
5. Sprinkle with garlic powder and parmesan and toss again.
6. Drizzle with more lemon juice.
7. Serve.

Variations & Ingredients Tips:

- Use olive oil or melted butter instead of lemon juice.
- Add red pepper flakes or paprika for spice.
- Substitute nutritional yeast for a dairy-free "cheesy" flavor.

Per Serving: Calories: 90; Total Fat: 1g; Saturated Fat: 0g; Cholesterol: 0mg; Sodium: 90mg; Total Carbs: 16g; Fiber: 2g; Sugars: 0g; Protein: 3g

Bacon-wrapped Asparagus

Servings: 4 | Prep Time: 10 Minutes | Cooking Time: 10 Minutes

Ingredients:

- 1 tablespoon extra-virgin olive oil
- ½ teaspoon sea salt
- ¼ cup grated Parmesan cheese
- 454g asparagus, ends trimmed
- 8 slices bacon

Directions:

1. Preheat the air fryer to 193°C/380°F.
2. In large bowl, mix together the olive oil, sea salt, and Parmesan cheese. Toss the asparagus in the olive oil mixture.
3. Evenly divide the asparagus into 8 bundles. Wrap 1 piece of bacon around each bundle, not overlapping the bacon but spreading it across the bundle.
4. Place the asparagus bundles into the air fryer basket, not touching. Work in batches as needed.
5. Cook for 8 minutes; check for doneness, and cook another 2 minutes.

Variations & Ingredients Tips:

- Brush the bundles with balsamic glaze before serving.
- Use prosciutto or pancetta instead of bacon.
- Add a sprinkle of brown sugar or honey to the olive oil mixture.

Per Serving: Calories: 220; Total Fat: 15g; Saturated Fat: 5g; Cholesterol: 25mg; Sodium: 600mg; Total Carbs: 6g; Fiber: 2g; Sugars: 2g; Protein: 16g

Cheesy Cauliflower Tart

Servings: 4 | Prep Time: 15 Minutes | Cooking Time: 40 Minutes

Ingredients:

- ½ cup cooked cauliflower, chopped
- ¼ cup grated Swiss cheese
- ¼ cup shredded cheddar
- 1 pie crust
- 2 eggs
- ¼ cup milk
- 6 black olives, chopped
- Salt and pepper to taste

Directions:

1. Preheat air fryer to 182°C/360°F.
2. Grease and line a tart tin with the pie crust. Trim the edges and prick lightly with a fork.
3. Whisk the eggs in a bowl until fluffy. Add the milk, cauliflower, salt, pepper, black olives, and half the cheddar and Swiss cheeses; stir to combine.
4. Carefully spoon the mixture into the pie crust and spread it level.
5. Bake in the air fryer for 15 minutes.
6. Slide the basket out and sprinkle the rest of the cheeses on top. Cook for another 5 minutes or until golden on the top and cooked through.
7. Leave to cool before serving.

Variations & Ingredients Tips:

- Add sautéed onions, spinach or mushrooms to the filling.
- Use a premade crust or make your own from scratch.
- Substitute feta or goat cheese for one of the cheese

varieties.

Per Serving: Calories: 280; Total Fat: 17g; Saturated Fat: 7g; Cholesterol: 100mg; Sodium: 420mg; Total Carbs: 20g; Fiber: 1g; Sugars: 2g; Protein: 11g

Dijon Roasted Purple Potatoes

Servings: 4 | Prep Time: 10 Minutes | Cooking Time: 25 Minutes

Ingredients:

- 454g purple potatoes, scrubbed and halved
- 1 tbsp olive oil
- 1 tsp Dijon mustard
- 1 tsp lemon juice
- 2 cloves garlic, minced
- Salt and pepper to taste
- 2 tbsp butter, melted
- 1 tbsp chopped cilantro
- 1 tsp fresh rosemary

Directions:

1. Mix the olive oil, mustard, garlic, lemon juice, pepper, salt and rosemary in a bowl. Chill covered until ready to use.
2. Preheat air fryer at 177°C/350°F.
3. Toss the potatoes, salt, pepper, and butter in a bowl.
4. Place potatoes in the frying basket, and Roast for 18-20 minutes, tossing once.
5. Transfer potatoes to a bowl. Drizzle with the dressing and toss to coat.
6. Garnish with cilantro to serve.

Variations & Ingredients Tips:

- Use Yukon gold or fingerling potatoes instead of purple.
- Add whole grain mustard or horseradish to the dressing.
- Sprinkle with crispy shallots or bacon bits.

Per Serving: Calories: 210; Total Fat: 12g; Saturated Fat: 5g; Cholesterol: 15mg; Sodium: 160mg; Total Carbs: 24g; Fiber: 3g; Sugars: 2g; Protein: 3g

Okra

Servings: 4 | Prep Time: 10 Minutes | Cooking Time: 12 Minutes

Ingredients:

- 198-227g fresh okra
- 1 egg
- 1 cup milk
- 1 cup breadcrumbs
- 1/2 teaspoon salt
- Oil for misting or cooking spray

Directions:

1. Remove stem ends from okra and cut into 25cm slices.
2. In a bowl, beat egg and milk. Add okra and stir to coat.
3. In a bag or container, mix breadcrumbs and salt.
4. Remove okra from egg mixture, letting excess drip off, and transfer to breadcrumb mixture.
5. Shake bag to fully coat okra.
6. Place coated okra in air fryer basket and mist with oil spray.
7. Cook at 199°C/390°F for 5 minutes. Shake and mist again.
8. Cook 5 more minutes. Shake, mist and cook 2 more minutes until crispy.

Variations & Ingredients Tips:

- Use panko breadcrumbs for extra crunch.
- Add cajun seasoning or hot sauce to the breadcrumb mix.
- Serve with a ranch or remoulade dipping sauce.

Per Serving: Calories: 189; Total Fat: 6g; Saturated Fat: 2g; Cholesterol: 60mg; Sodium: 487mg; Total Carbohydrates: 29g; Dietary Fiber: 4g; Total Sugars: 6g; Protein: 8g

Smooth & Silky Cauliflower Purée

Servings: 4 | Prep Time: 10 Minutes | Cooking Time: 25 Minutes

Ingredients:

- 1 head cauliflower, cut into florets
- 1 rutabaga, diced
- 4 tablespoons butter, divided
- Salt and pepper to taste
- 3 cloves garlic, peeled
- 55 g cream cheese, softened
- 120 ml milk
- 1 teaspoon dried thyme

Directions:

1. Preheat air fryer to 180°C/350°F.
2. Combine cauliflower, rutabaga, 2 tablespoons of butter, and salt to taste in a bowl.
3. Add veggie mixture to the frying basket and Air Fry for

10 minutes, tossing once.
4. Put in garlic and Air Fry for 5 more minutes.
5. Let them cool a bit, then transfer them to a blender.
6. Blend them along with 2 tablespoons of butter, salt, black pepper, cream cheese, thyme and milk until smooth.
7. Serve immediately.

Variations & Ingredients Tips:

- Use different herbs, such as rosemary or sage, for a unique flavor profile.
- Add some grated Parmesan cheese or nutritional yeast for a cheesy flavor.
- For a vegan version, replace the butter and cream cheese with plant-based alternatives and use unsweetened almond milk or coconut milk.

Per Serving: Calories: 230; Total Fat: 19g; Saturated Fat: 12g; Cholesterol: 50mg; Sodium: 220mg; Total Carbs: 12g; Fiber: 4g; Sugars: 5g; Protein: 5g

Blistered Tomatoes

Servings: 20 | Prep Time: 5 Minutes | Cooking Time: 15 Minutes

Ingredients:

- 680g Cherry or grape tomatoes
- Olive oil spray
- 1½ teaspoons Balsamic vinegar
- ¼ teaspoon Table salt
- ¼ teaspoon Ground black pepper

Directions:

1. Put the basket in a drawer-style air fryer, or a baking tray in the lower third of a toaster oven–style air fryer. Place a 15cm round cake pan in the basket or on the tray for a small batch, a 18cm round cake pan for a medium batch, or a 20cm round cake pan for a large one. Heat the air fryer to 200°C/400°F with the pan in the basket. When the machine is at temperature, keep heating the pan for 5 minutes more.
2. Place the tomatoes in a large bowl, coat them with the olive oil spray, toss gently, then spritz a couple of times more, tossing after each spritz, until the tomatoes are glistening.
3. Pour the tomatoes into the cake pan and air-fry undisturbed for 10 minutes, or until they split and begin to brown.
4. Use kitchen tongs and a nonstick-safe spatula, or silicone baking mitts, to remove the cake pan from the basket. Toss the hot tomatoes with the vinegar, salt, and pepper. Cool in the pan for a few minutes before serving.

Variations & Ingredients Tips:

- Add minced garlic and fresh herbs like basil before serving.
- Drizzle with balsamic reduction or pesto after cooking.
- Serve over toasted bread as a bruschetta topping.

Per Serving: Calories: 15; Total Fat: 0g; Saturated Fat: 0g; Cholesterol: 0mg; Sodium: 20mg; Total Carbs: 3g; Fiber: 1g; Sugars: 2g; Protein: 1g

Parmesan Garlic Fries

Servings: 4 | Prep Time: 10 Minutes | Cooking Time: 20 Minutes

Ingredients:

- 2 medium Yukon gold potatoes, washed
- 1 tablespoon extra-virgin olive oil
- 1 garlic clove, minced
- 2 tablespoons finely grated parmesan cheese
- 1/4 teaspoon black pepper
- 1/4 teaspoon salt
- 1 tablespoon freshly chopped parsley

Directions:

1. Preheat the air fryer to 200°C/400°F.
2. Slice the potatoes into 6mm thick fry strips.
3. In a bowl, toss the potatoes with olive oil, garlic, parmesan, pepper and salt.
4. Place the fries into the air fryer basket and cook for 4 minutes, shake basket and cook 4 more minutes.
5. Remove and toss with chopped parsley.
6. Serve warm.

Variations & Ingredients Tips:

- Use russet or sweet potatoes instead of Yukon gold.
- Add garlic powder or Italian seasoning for extra flavor.
- Serve with marinara or ranch dressing for dipping.

Per Serving: Calories: 123; Total Fat: 5g; Saturated Fat: 1g; Cholesterol: 2mg; Sodium: 259mg; Total Carbohydrates: 17g; Dietary Fiber: 2g; Total Sugars: 1g; Protein: 3g

Toasted Choco-nuts

Servings: 2 | Prep Time: 5 Minutes | Cooking Time: 10 Minutes

Ingredients:

- 2 cups almonds
- 2 teaspoons maple syrup
- 2 tablespoons cacao powder

Directions:

1. Preheat air fryer to 180°C/350°F.
2. Distribute the almonds in a single layer in the frying basket and Bake for 3 minutes.
3. Shake the basket and Bake for another 1 minute until golden brown.
4. Remove them to a bowl. Drizzle with maple syrup and toss.
5. Sprinkle with cacao powder and toss until well coated.
6. Let cool completely.
7. Store in a container at room temperature for up to 2 weeks or in the fridge for up to a month.

Variations & Ingredients Tips:

- Use different types of nuts, such as cashews or pecans, for a variety of flavors and textures.
- Add some ground cinnamon or vanilla extract for extra flavor.
- For a savory version, replace the maple syrup and cacao powder with olive oil and your favorite spice blend.

Per Serving: Calories: 580; Total Fat: 51g; Saturated Fat: 4g; Cholesterol: 0mg; Sodium: 0mg; Total Carbs: 27g; Fiber: 13g; Sugars: 9g; Protein: 21g

Classic Stuffed Shells

Servings: 4 | Prep Time: 15 Minutes | Cooking Time: 35 Minutes

Ingredients:

- 1 cup chopped spinach, cooked
- 1 cup shredded mozzarella
- 4 cooked jumbo shells
- 1 tsp dry oregano
- 1 cup ricotta cheese
- 1 egg, beaten
- 1 cup marinara sauce
- 1 tbsp basil leaves

Directions:

1. Preheat air fryer to 182°C/360°F.
2. Place the beaten egg, oregano, ricotta, mozzarella, and chopped spinach in a bowl and mix until combined.
3. Fill the mixture into the cooked pasta shells.
4. Spread half of the marinara sauce on a baking pan, then place the stuffed shells over the sauce.
5. Spoon the remaining marinara sauce over the shells.
6. Bake in the air fryer for 25 minutes or until crispy outside with gooey cheese inside.
7. Sprinkle with basil leaves and serve warm.

Variations & Ingredients Tips:

- Use a spinach and artichoke or meat filling instead.
- Top with extra mozzarella or parmesan before baking.
- Make it vegetarian by using a plant-based ricotta.

Per Serving: Calories: 375; Total Fat: 19g; Saturated Fat: 10g; Cholesterol: 120mg; Sodium: 710mg; Total Carbs: 29g; Fiber: 4g; Sugars: 7g; Protein: 24g

Street Corn

Servings: 4 | Prep Time: 5 Minutes | Cooking Time: 10 Minutes

Ingredients:

- 1 tablespoon butter
- 4 ears corn
- 80 ml plain Greek yogurt
- 2 tablespoons Parmesan cheese
- ½ teaspoon paprika
- ½ teaspoon garlic powder
- ¼ teaspoon salt
- ¼ teaspoon black pepper
- 60 ml finely chopped cilantro

Directions:

1. Preheat the air fryer to 200°C/400°F.
2. In a medium microwave-safe bowl, melt the butter in the microwave. Lightly brush the outside of the ears of corn with the melted butter.
3. Place the corn into the air fryer basket and cook for 5 minutes, flip the corn, and cook another 5 minutes.
4. Meanwhile, in a medium bowl, mix the yogurt, cheese, paprika, garlic powder, salt, and pepper. Set aside.
5. Carefully remove the corn from the air fryer and let cool 3 minutes. Brush the outside edges with the yogurt mixture and top with fresh chopped cilantro. Serve immediately.

Variations & Ingredients Tips:

- Use mayonnaise or sour cream instead of Greek yogurt for a richer flavor.
- Add some chili powder or cayenne pepper for a spicy kick.

- Sprinkle some crumbled feta cheese or cotija cheese on top for a salty and tangy flavor.

Per Serving: Calories: 140; Total Fat: 6g; Saturated Fat: 3g; Cholesterol: 10mg; Sodium: 230mg; Total Carbs: 19g; Fiber: 2g; Sugars: 6g; Protein: 5g

Southwestern Sweet Potato Wedges

Servings: 4 | Prep Time: 10 Minutes | Cooking Time: 30 Minutes

Ingredients:

- 2 sweet potatoes, peeled and cut into 1.25 cm wedges
- 2 teaspoons olive oil
- 2 tablespoons cornstarch
- 1 teaspoon garlic powder
- ¼ teaspoon ground allspice
- ¼ teaspoon paprika
- ⅛ teaspoon cayenne pepper

Directions:

1. Preheat air fryer to 200°C/400°F.
2. Place the sweet potatoes in a bowl. Add some olive oil and toss to coat, then transfer to the frying basket.
3. Roast for 8 minutes.
4. Sprinkle the potatoes with cornstarch, garlic powder, allspice, paprika, and cayenne, then toss.
5. Put the potatoes back into the fryer and Roast for 12-17 more minutes. Shake the basket a couple of times while cooking. The potatoes should be golden and crispy.
6. Serve warm.

Variations & Ingredients Tips:

- Use different spices, such as cumin, chili powder, or smoked paprika, for a unique flavor profile.
- Add some chopped fresh herbs, such as cilantro or parsley, for a fresh and bright flavor.
- Serve the sweet potato wedges with a dipping sauce, such as chipotle mayo or avocado crema.

Per Serving: Calories: 110; Total Fat: 2.5g; Saturated Fat: 0g; Cholesterol: 0mg; Sodium: 45mg; Total Carbs: 22g; Fiber: 3g; Sugars: 4g; Protein: 2g

Sandwiches And Burgers Recipes

White Bean Veggie Burgers

Servings: 3 | Prep Time: 15 Minutes | Cooking Time: 13 Minutes

Ingredients:

- 320 grams Drained and rinsed canned white beans
- 3 tablespoons Rolled oats (not quick-cooking or steel-cut; gluten-free, if a concern)
- 3 tablespoons Chopped walnuts
- 2 teaspoons Olive oil
- 2 teaspoons Lemon juice
- 1½ teaspoons Dijon mustard (gluten-free, if a concern)
- ¾ teaspoon Dried sage leaves
- ¼ teaspoon Table salt
- Olive oil spray
- 3 Whole-wheat buns or gluten-free whole-grain buns (if a concern), split open

Directions:

1. Preheat the air fryer to 200°C/400°F.
2. Place the beans, oats, walnuts, oil, lemon juice, mustard, sage, and salt in a food processor. Cover and pro-

cess to make a coarse paste that will hold its shape, about like wet sugar-cookie dough, stopping the machine to scrape down the inside of the canister at least once.

3. Scrape down and remove the blade. With clean and wet hands, form the bean paste into two 10-cm patties for the small batch, three 10-cm patties for the medium, or four 10-cm patties for the large batch. Generously coat the patties on both sides with olive oil spray.
4. Set them in the basket with some space between them and air-fry undisturbed for 12 minutes, or until lightly brown and crisp at the edges. The tops of the burgers will feel firm to the touch.
5. Use a nonstick-safe spatula, and perhaps a flatware fork for balance, to transfer the burgers to a cutting board. Set the buns cut side down in the basket in one layer (working in batches as necessary) and air-fry undisturbed for 1 minute, to toast a bit and warm up. Serve the burgers warm in the buns.

Variations & Ingredients Tips:

- Use black beans, chickpeas, or lentils instead of white beans for a different flavor and color.
- Add grated carrots, zucchini, or beets to the burger mixture for extra nutrition and texture.
- Serve with your favorite burger toppings like lettuce, tomato, onion, and pickles.

Per Serving (1 burger): Calories: 350; Cholesterol: 0mg; Total Fat: 13g; Saturated Fat: 1g; Sodium: 520mg; Total Carbohydrates: 48g; Dietary Fiber: 9g; Total Sugars: 4g; Protein: 14g

Thanksgiving Turkey Sandwiches

Servings: 3 | Prep Time: 15 Minutes | Cooking Time: 10 Minutes

Ingredients:

- 1½ cups Herb-seasoned stuffing mix (not cornbread-style; gluten-free, if a concern)
- 1 Large egg white(s)
- 2 tablespoons Water
- 3 140- to 170-gram turkey breast cutlets
- Vegetable oil spray
- 4½ tablespoons Purchased cranberry sauce, preferably whole berry
- ⅛ teaspoon Ground cinnamon
- ⅛ teaspoon Ground dried ginger
- 4½ tablespoons Regular, low-fat, or fat-free mayonnaise (gluten-free, if a concern)
- 6 tablespoons Shredded Brussels sprouts
- 3 Kaiser rolls (gluten-free, if a concern), split open

Directions:

1. Preheat the air fryer to 190°C/375°F.
2. Put the stuffing mix in a heavy zip-closed bag, seal it, lay it flat on your counter, and roll a rolling pin over the bag to crush the stuffing mix to the consistency of rough sand. (Or you can pulse the stuffing mix to the desired consistency in a food processor.)
3. Set up and fill two shallow soup plates or small pie plates on your counter: one for the egg white(s), whisked with the water until foamy; and one for the ground stuffing mix.
4. Dip a cutlet in the egg white mixture, coating both sides and letting any excess egg white slip back into the rest. Set the cutlet in the ground stuffing mix and coat it evenly on both sides, pressing gently to coat well on both sides. Lightly coat the cutlet on both sides with vegetable oil spray, set it aside, and continue dipping and coating the remaining cutlets in the same way.
5. Set the cutlets in the basket and air-fry undisturbed for 10 minutes, or until crisp and brown. Use kitchen tongs to transfer the cutlets to a wire rack to cool for a few minutes.
6. Meanwhile, stir the cranberry sauce with the cinnamon and ginger in a small bowl. Mix the shredded Brussels sprouts and mayonnaise in a second bowl until the vegetable is evenly coated.
7. Build the sandwiches by spreading about 1½ tablespoons of the cranberry mixture on the cut side of the bottom half of each roll. Set a cutlet on top, then spread about 3 tablespoons of the Brussels sprouts mixture evenly over the cutlet. Set the other half of the roll on top and serve warm.

Variations & Ingredients Tips:

- Use leftover roasted turkey instead of turkey cutlets for a post-Thanksgiving sandwich.
- Substitute Brussels sprouts with shredded cabbage or kale for a different texture and flavor.
- Add a slice of brie or provolone cheese to the sandwich for extra creaminess.

Per Serving: Calories: 530; Cholesterol: 75mg; Total Fat: 22g; Saturated Fat: 4g; Sodium: 1180mg; Total Carbohydrates: 53g; Dietary Fiber: 4g; Total Sugars: 15g; Protein: 33g

Philly Cheesesteak Sandwiches

Servings: 3 | Prep Time: 10 Minutes | Cooking Time: 9 Minutes

Ingredients:

- 340 grams Shaved beef

- 1 tablespoon Worcestershire sauce (gluten-free, if a concern)
- ¼ teaspoon Garlic powder
- ¼ teaspoon Mild paprika
- 6 tablespoons (45 grams) Frozen bell pepper strips (do not thaw)
- 2 slices, broken into rings Very thin yellow or white medium onion slice(s)
- 170 grams (6 to 8 slices) Provolone cheese slices
- 3 Long soft rolls such as hero, hoagie, or Italian sub rolls, or hot dog buns (gluten-free, if a concern), split open lengthwise

Directions:

1. Preheat the air fryer to 200°C/400°F.
2. When the machine is at temperature, spread the shaved beef in the basket, leaving a 1.25-cm perimeter around the meat for good air flow. Sprinkle the meat with the Worcestershire sauce, paprika, and garlic powder. Spread the peppers and onions on top of the meat.
3. Air-fry undisturbed for 6 minutes, or until cooked through. Set the cheese on top of the meat. Continue air-frying undisturbed for 3 minutes, or until the cheese has melted.
4. Use kitchen tongs to divide the meat and cheese layers in the basket between the rolls or buns. Serve hot.

Variations & Ingredients Tips:

▶ Use thinly sliced ribeye or sirloin steak instead of shaved beef for a more traditional texture.
▶ Add sliced mushrooms to the pepper and onion mixture for extra flavor and nutrition.
▶ Substitute provolone with American cheese or Cheez Whiz for a classic Philly taste.

Per Serving: Calories: 620; Cholesterol: 135mg; Total Fat: 32g; Saturated Fat: 15g; Sodium: 1320mg; Total Carbohydrates: 38g; Dietary Fiber: 2g; Total Sugars: 5g; Protein: 48g

Lamb Burgers

Servings: 3 | Prep Time: 15 Minutes | Cooking Time: 17 Minutes

Ingredients:

- 510 grams Ground lamb
- 3 tablespoons Crumbled feta
- 1 teaspoon Minced garlic
- 1 teaspoon Tomato paste
- ¾ teaspoon Ground coriander
- ¾ teaspoon Ground dried ginger
- Up to ⅛ teaspoon Cayenne
- Up to a ⅛ teaspoon Table salt (optional)
- 3 Kaiser rolls or hamburger buns (gluten-free, if a concern), split open

Directions:

1. Preheat the air fryer to 190°C/375°F.
2. Gently mix the ground lamb, feta, garlic, tomato paste, coriander, ginger, cayenne, and salt (if using) in a bowl until well combined, trying to keep the bits of cheese intact. Form this mixture into two 15-cm patties for the small batch, three 12.5-cm patties for the medium, or four 12.5-cm patties for the large.
3. Set the patties in the basket in one layer and air-fry undisturbed for 16 minutes, or until an instant-read meat thermometer inserted into one burger registers 70°C/160°F. (The cheese is not an issue with the temperature probe in this recipe as it was for the Inside-Out Cheeseburgers, because the feta is so well mixed into the ground meat.)
4. Use a nonstick-safe spatula, and perhaps a flatware fork for balance, to transfer the burgers to a cutting board. Set the buns cut side down in the basket in one layer (working in batches as necessary) and air-fry undisturbed for 1 minute, to toast a bit and warm up. Serve the burgers warm in the buns.

Variations & Ingredients Tips:

▶ Substitute feta with goat cheese or crumbled blue cheese for a different flavor profile.
▶ Add finely chopped mint or parsley to the lamb mixture for a fresh, herbal taste.
▶ Serve with tzatziki sauce, sliced cucumbers, and red onions for a Greek-inspired burger.

Per Serving (1 burger): Calories: 560; Cholesterol: 140mg; Total Fat: 34g; Saturated Fat: 15g; Sodium: 580mg; Total Carbohydrates: 25g; Dietary Fiber: 1g; Total Sugars: 3g; Protein: 38g

Crunchy Falafel Balls

Servings: 8 | Prep Time: 15 Minutes | Cooking Time: 16 Minutes

Ingredients:

- 600 grams Drained and rinsed canned chickpeas
- 60 grams Olive oil
- 3 tablespoons All-purpose flour
- 1½ teaspoons Dried oregano

- 1½ teaspoons Dried sage leaves
- 1½ teaspoons Dried thyme
- ¾ teaspoon Table salt
- Olive oil spray

Directions:

1. Preheat the air fryer to 200°C/400°F.
2. Place the chickpeas, olive oil, flour, oregano, sage, thyme, and salt in a food processor. Cover and process into a paste, stopping the machine at least once to scrape down the inside of the canister.
3. Scrape down and remove the blade. Using clean, wet hands, form 2 tablespoons of the paste into a ball, then continue making 9 more balls for a small batch, 15 more for a medium one, and 19 more for a large batch. Generously coat the balls in olive oil spray.
4. Set the balls in the basket in one layer with a little space between them and air-fry undisturbed for 16 minutes, or until well browned and crisp.
5. Dump the contents of the basket onto a wire rack. Cool for 5 minutes before serving.

Variations & Ingredients Tips:

- Add minced garlic, onion, or herbs like parsley or cilantro for extra flavor.
- Serve with tahini sauce, hummus, or tzatziki for dipping.
- Make a falafel sandwich by stuffing pita bread with falafel balls, lettuce, tomato, and sauce.

Per Serving (2 falafel balls): Calories: 170; Cholesterol: 0mg; Total Fat: 9g; Saturated Fat: 1g; Sodium: 230mg; Total Carbohydrates: 18g; Dietary Fiber: 4g; Total Sugars: 2g; Protein: 5g

Reuben Sandwiches

Servings: 2 | Prep Time: 10 Minutes | Cooking Time: 11 Minutes

Ingredients:

- 225 grams Sliced deli corned beef
- 4 teaspoons Regular or low-fat mayonnaise (not fat-free)
- 4 Rye bread slices
- 2 tablespoons plus 2 teaspoons Russian dressing
- ½ cup Purchased sauerkraut, squeezed by the handful over the sink to get rid of excess moisture
- 55 grams (2 to 4 slices) Swiss cheese slices (optional)

Directions:

1. Set the corned beef in the basket, slip the basket into the machine, and heat the air fryer to 200°C/400°F. Air-fry undisturbed for 3 minutes from the time the basket is put in the machine, just to warm up the meat.
2. Use kitchen tongs to transfer the corned beef to a cutting board. Spread 1 teaspoon mayonnaise on one side of each slice of rye bread, rubbing the mayonnaise into the bread with a small flatware knife.
3. Place the bread slices mayonnaise side down on a cutting board. Spread the Russian dressing over the "dry" side of each slice. For one sandwich, top one slice of bread with the corned beef, sauerkraut, and cheese (if using). For two sandwiches, top two slices of bread each with half of the corned beef, sauerkraut, and cheese (if using). Close the sandwiches with the remaining bread, setting it mayonnaise side up on top.
4. Set the sandwich(es) in the basket and air-fry undisturbed for 8 minutes, or until browned and crunchy.
5. Use a nonstick-safe spatula, and perhaps a flatware fork for balance, to transfer the sandwich(es) to a cutting board. Cool for 2 or 3 minutes before slicing in half and serving.

Variations & Ingredients Tips:

- Substitute corned beef with pastrami for a classic New York deli taste.
- Use Thousand Island dressing instead of Russian dressing for a tangy, sweet flavor.
- Add sliced dill pickles or mustard to the sandwich for extra zing.

Per Serving (1 sandwich): Calories: 520; Cholesterol: 75mg; Total Fat: 30g; Saturated Fat: 9g; Sodium: 2020mg; Total Carbohydrates: 36g; Dietary Fiber: 4g; Total Sugars: 6g; Protein: 29g

Chicken Spiedies

Servings: 3 | Prep Time: 15 Minutes (plus Marinating Time) | Cooking Time: 12 Minutes

Ingredients:

- 570 grams Boneless skinless chicken thighs, trimmed of any fat blobs and cut into 5-cm pieces
- 3 tablespoons Red wine vinegar
- 2 tablespoons Olive oil
- 2 tablespoons Minced fresh mint leaves
- 2 tablespoons Minced fresh parsley leaves
- 2 teaspoons Minced fresh dill fronds
- ¾ teaspoon Fennel seeds
- ¾ teaspoon Table salt

- Up to a ¼ teaspoon Red pepper flakes
- 3 Long soft rolls, such as hero, hoagie, or Italian sub rolls (gluten-free, if a concern), split open lengthwise
- 4½ tablespoons Regular or low-fat mayonnaise (not fat-free; gluten-free, if a concern)
- 1½ tablespoons Distilled white vinegar
- 1½ teaspoons Ground black pepper

Directions:

1. Mix the chicken, vinegar, oil, mint, parsley, dill, fennel seeds, salt, and red pepper flakes in a zip-closed plastic bag. Seal, gently massage the marinade ingredients into the meat, and refrigerate for at least 2 hours or up to 6 hours. (Longer than that and the meat can turn rubbery.)
2. Set the plastic bag out on the counter (to make the contents a little less frigid). Preheat the air fryer to 200°C/400°F.
3. When the machine is at temperature, use kitchen tongs to set the chicken thighs in the basket (discard any remaining marinade) and air-fry undisturbed for 6 minutes. Turn the thighs over and continue air-frying undisturbed for 6 minutes more, until well browned, cooked through, and even a little crunchy.
4. Dump the contents of the basket onto a wire rack and cool for 2 or 3 minutes. Divide the chicken evenly between the rolls. Whisk the mayonnaise, vinegar, and black pepper in a small bowl until smooth. Drizzle this sauce over the chicken pieces in the rolls.

Variations & Ingredients Tips:

- Use chicken breast instead of thighs for a leaner option.
- Substitute the herbs with your favorite combination, such as basil, oregano, or thyme.
- Add sliced onions or pickled vegetables for extra crunch and tanginess.

Per Serving: Calories: 710; Cholesterol: 200mg; Total Fat: 44g; Saturated Fat: 8g; Sodium: 1240mg; Total Carbohydrates: 37g; Dietary Fiber: 2g; Total Sugars: 4g; Protein: 45g

Perfect Burgers

Servings: 3 | Prep Time: 10 Minutes | Cooking Time: 13 Minutes

Ingredients:

- 510 grams 90% lean ground beef
- 1½ tablespoons Worcestershire sauce (gluten-free, if a concern)
- ½ teaspoon Ground black pepper
- 3 Hamburger buns (gluten-free if a concern), split open

Directions:

1. Preheat the air fryer to 190°C/375°F.
2. Gently mix the ground beef, Worcestershire sauce, and pepper in a bowl until well combined but preserving as much of the meat's fibers as possible. Divide this mixture into two 15-cm patties for the small batch, three 12.5-cm patties for the medium, or four 12.5-cm patties for the large. Make a thumbprint indentation in the center of each patty, about halfway through the meat.
3. Set the patties in the basket in one layer with some space between them. Air-fry undisturbed for 10 minutes, or until an instant-read meat thermometer inserted into the center of a burger registers 70°C/160°F (a medium-well burger). You may need to add 2 minutes cooking time if the air fryer is at 180°C/360°F.
4. Use a nonstick-safe spatula, and perhaps a flatware fork for balance, to transfer the burgers to a cutting board. Set the buns cut side down in the basket in one layer (working in batches as necessary) and air-fry undisturbed for 1 minute, to toast a bit and warm up. Serve the burgers in the warm buns.

Variations & Ingredients Tips:

- Mix in finely chopped onions, garlic, or herbs to the burger mixture for extra flavor.
- Use a mixture of ground beef and ground pork or lamb for a juicier, more flavorful burger.
- Top burgers with your favorite cheese, bacon, avocado, or sautéed mushrooms.

Per Serving (1 burger): Calories: 420; Cholesterol: 105mg; Total Fat: 22g; Saturated Fat: 8g; Sodium: 460mg; Total Carbohydrates: 23g; Dietary Fiber: 1g; Total Sugars: 3g; Protein: 34g

Mexican Cheeseburgers

Servings: 4 | Prep Time: 20 Minutes | Cooking Time: 22 Minutes

Ingredients:

- 570 grams ground beef
- ¼ cup finely chopped onion
- ½ cup crushed yellow corn tortilla chips
- 1 (35-gram) packet taco seasoning
- ¼ cup canned diced green chilies
- 1 egg, lightly beaten
- 115 grams pepper jack cheese, grated
- 4 (30-cm) flour tortillas

- shredded lettuce, sour cream, guacamole, salsa (for topping)

Directions:

1. Combine the ground beef, minced onion, crushed tortilla chips, taco seasoning, green chilies, and egg in a large bowl. Mix thoroughly until combined – your hands are good tools for this. Divide the meat into four equal portions and shape each portion into an oval-shaped burger.
2. Preheat the air fryer to 190°C/370°F.
3. Air-fry the burgers for 18 minutes, turning them over halfway through the cooking time. Divide the cheese between the burgers, lower fryer to 170°C/340°F and air-fry for an additional 4 minutes to melt the cheese. (This will give you a burger that is medium-well. If you prefer your cheeseburger medium-rare, shorten the cooking time to about 15 minutes and then add the cheese and proceed with the recipe.)
4. While the burgers are cooking, warm the tortillas wrapped in aluminum foil in a 175°C/350°F oven, or in a skillet with a little oil over medium-high heat for a couple of minutes. Keep the tortillas warm until the burgers are ready.
5. To assemble the burgers, spread sour cream over three quarters of the tortillas and top each with some shredded lettuce and salsa. Place the Mexican cheeseburgers on the lettuce and top with guacamole. Fold the tortillas around the burger, starting with the bottom and then folding the sides in over the top. (A little sour cream can help hold the seam of the tortilla together.) Serve immediately.

Variations & Ingredients Tips:

- Use ground turkey or chicken for a leaner burger option.
- Substitute pepper jack cheese with Monterey Jack or cheddar cheese if preferred.
- Add sliced jalapeños or hot sauce to the burger mixture for extra heat.

Per Serving (1 burger): Calories: 780; Cholesterol: 165mg; Total Fat: 44g; Saturated Fat: 18g; Sodium: 1480mg; Total Carbohydrates: 51g; Dietary Fiber: 4g; Total Sugars: 4g; Protein: 46g

Thai-style Pork Sliders

Servings: 4 | Prep Time: 15 Minutes | Cooking Time: 15 Minutes

Ingredients:

- 310 grams Ground pork
- 2½ tablespoons Very thinly sliced scallions, white and green parts
- 4 teaspoons Minced peeled fresh ginger
- 2½ teaspoons Fish sauce (gluten-free, if a concern)
- 2 teaspoons Thai curry paste (see the headnote; gluten-free, if a concern)
- 2 teaspoons Light brown sugar
- ¾ teaspoon Ground black pepper
- 4 Slider buns (gluten-free, if a concern)

Directions:

1. Preheat the air fryer to 190°C/375°F.
2. Gently mix the pork, scallions, ginger, fish sauce, curry paste, brown sugar, and black pepper in a bowl until well combined. With clean, wet hands, form about 80 grams of the pork mixture into a slider about 6.5-cm in diameter. Repeat until you use up all the meat—3 sliders for the small batch, 4 for the medium, and 6 for the large. (Keep wetting your hands to help the patties adhere.)
3. When the machine is at temperature, set the sliders in the basket in one layer. Air-fry undisturbed for 14 minutes, or until the sliders are golden brown and caramelized at their edges and an instant-read meat thermometer inserted into the center of a slider registers 70°C/160°F.
4. Use a nonstick-safe spatula, and perhaps a flatware fork for balance, to transfer the sliders to a cutting board. Set the buns cut side down in the basket in one layer (working in batches as necessary) and air-fry undisturbed for 1 minute, to toast a bit and warm up. Serve the sliders warm in the buns.

Variations & Ingredients Tips:

- Use ground chicken or turkey for a leaner slider option.
- Substitute Thai curry paste with red curry paste or green curry paste for a different flavor profile.
- Serve with pickled vegetables, cilantro, and sriracha mayonnaise for extra Thai-inspired toppings.

Per Serving (1 slider): Calories: 240; Cholesterol: 65mg; Total Fat: 13g; Saturated Fat: 4g; Sodium: 490mg; Total Carbohydrates: 18g; Dietary Fiber: 1g; Total Sugars: 4g; Protein: 15g

Inside Out Cheeseburgers

Servings: 2 | Prep Time: 15 Minutes | Cooking Time: 20 Minutes

Ingredients:

- 340 grams lean ground beef

- 3 tablespoons minced onion
- 4 teaspoons ketchup
- 2 teaspoons yellow mustard
- salt and freshly ground black pepper
- 4 slices of Cheddar cheese, broken into smaller pieces
- 8 hamburger dill pickle chips

Directions:

1. Combine the ground beef, minced onion, ketchup, mustard, salt and pepper in a large bowl. Mix well to thoroughly combine the ingredients. Divide the meat into four equal portions.
2. To make the stuffed burgers, flatten each portion of meat into a thin patty. Place 4 pickle chips and half of the cheese onto the center of two of the patties, leaving a rim around the edge of the patty exposed. Place the remaining two patties on top of the first and press the meat together firmly, sealing the edges tightly. With the burgers on a flat surface, press the sides of the burger with the palm of your hand to create a straight edge. This will help keep the stuffing inside the burger while it cooks.
3. Preheat the air fryer to 190°C/370°F.
4. Place the burgers inside the air fryer basket and air-fry for 20 minutes, flipping the burgers over halfway through the cooking time.
5. Serve the cheeseburgers on buns with lettuce and tomato.

Variations & Ingredients Tips:

- Use different types of cheese like Swiss, pepper jack, or blue cheese for a unique flavor.
- Add crispy bacon pieces or sautéed mushrooms to the stuffing for extra richness.
- Brush the burgers with a mixture of melted butter and minced garlic before cooking for added flavor.

Per Serving (1 burger): Calories: 510; Cholesterol: 145mg; Total Fat: 32g; Saturated Fat: 14g; Sodium: 780mg; Total Carbohydrates: 12g; Dietary Fiber: 1g; Total Sugars: 6g; Protein: 42g

Chicken Saltimbocca Sandwiches

Servings: 3 | Prep Time: 10 Minutes | Cooking Time: 11 Minutes

Ingredients:

- 3 140to 170-gram boneless skinless chicken breasts
- 6 Thin prosciutto slices
- 6 Provolone cheese slices
- 3 Long soft rolls, such as hero, hoagie, or Italian sub rolls (gluten-free, if a concern), split open lengthwise
- 3 tablespoons Pesto, purchased or homemade (see the headnote)

Directions:

1. Preheat the air fryer to 200°C/400°F.
2. Wrap each chicken breast with 2 prosciutto slices, spiraling the prosciutto around the breast and overlapping the slices a bit to cover the breast. The prosciutto will stick to the chicken more readily than bacon does.
3. When the machine is at temperature, set the wrapped chicken breasts in the basket and air-fry undisturbed for 10 minutes, or until the prosciutto is frizzled and the chicken is cooked through.
4. Overlap 2 cheese slices on each breast. Air-fry undisturbed for 1 minute, or until melted. Take the basket out of the machine.
5. Smear the insides of the rolls with the pesto, then use kitchen tongs to put a wrapped and cheesy chicken breast in each roll.

Variations & Ingredients Tips:

- Use fresh mozzarella instead of provolone for a creamier texture.
- Add sliced tomatoes or roasted red peppers for extra flavor and nutrition.
- Substitute prosciutto with ham or bacon if desired.

Per Serving: Calories: 630; Cholesterol: 125mg; Total Fat: 32g; Saturated Fat: 11g; Sodium: 1580mg; Total Carbohydrates: 38g; Dietary Fiber: 2g; Total Sugars: 4g; Protein: 48g

Chicken Club Sandwiches

Servings: 3 | Prep Time: 15 Minutes | Cooking Time: 15 Minutes

Ingredients:

- 3 140- to 170-gram boneless skinless chicken breasts
- 6 Thick-cut bacon strips (gluten-free, if a concern)
- 3 Long soft rolls, such as hero, hoagie, or Italian sub rolls (gluten-free, if a concern)
- 3 tablespoons Regular, low-fat, or fat-free mayonnaise (gluten-free, if a concern)
- 3 Lettuce leaves, preferably romaine or iceberg

- 6 6-mm-thick tomato slices

Directions:

1. Preheat the air fryer to 190°C/375°F.
2. Wrap each chicken breast with 2 strips of bacon, spiraling the bacon around the meat, slightly overlapping the strips on each revolution. Start the second strip of bacon farther down the breast but on a line with the start of the first strip so they both end at a lined-up point on the chicken breast.
3. When the machine is at temperature, set the wrapped breasts bacon-seam side down in the basket with space between them. Air-fry undisturbed for 12 minutes, until the bacon is browned, crisp, and cooked through and an instant-read meat thermometer inserted into the center of a breast registers 75°C/165°F. You may need to add 2 minutes in the air fryer if the temperature is at 70°C/160°F.
4. Use kitchen tongs to transfer the breasts to a wire rack. Split the rolls open lengthwise and set them cut side down in the basket. Air-fry for 1 minute, or until warmed through.
5. Use kitchen tongs to transfer the rolls to a cutting board. Spread 1 tablespoon mayonnaise on the cut side of one half of each roll. Top with a chicken breast, lettuce leaf, and tomato slice. Serve warm.

Variations & Ingredients Tips:

- Use turkey bacon for a lower-fat option.
- Add sliced avocado or pickled onions for extra flavor and texture.
- Toast the rolls before assembling the sandwiches for a crispy texture.

Per Serving: Calories: 640; Cholesterol: 110mg; Total Fat: 34g; Saturated Fat: 9g; Sodium: 1180mg; Total Carbohydrates: 44g; Dietary Fiber: 2g; Total Sugars: 5g; Protein: 42g

Asian Glazed Meatballs

Servings: 4 | Prep Time: 15 Minutes | Cooking Time: 10 Minutes

Ingredients:

- 1 large shallot, finely chopped
- 2 cloves garlic, minced
- 1 tablespoon grated fresh ginger
- 2 teaspoons fresh thyme, finely chopped
- 1½ cups brown mushrooms, very finely chopped (a food processor works well here)
- 2 tablespoons soy sauce
- freshly ground black pepper
- ½ kg ground beef
- ¼ kg ground pork
- 3 egg yolks
- 1 cup Thai sweet chili sauce (spring roll sauce)
- ¼ cup toasted sesame seeds
- 2 scallions, sliced

Directions:

1. Combine the shallot, garlic, ginger, thyme, mushrooms, soy sauce, freshly ground black pepper, ground beef and pork, and egg yolks in a bowl and mix the ingredients together. Gently shape the mixture into 24 balls, about the size of a golf ball.
2. Preheat the air fryer to 190°C/380°F.
3. Working in batches, air-fry the meatballs for 8 minutes, turning the meatballs over halfway through the cooking time. Drizzle some of the Thai sweet chili sauce on top of each meatball and return the basket to the air fryer, air-frying for another 2 minutes. Reserve the remaining Thai sweet chili sauce for serving.
4. As soon as the meatballs are done, sprinkle with toasted sesame seeds and transfer them to a serving platter. Scatter the scallions around and serve warm.

Variations & Ingredients Tips:

- Use a food processor to finely chop the mushrooms for better texture in the meatballs.
- Work in batches when air frying the meatballs to ensure even cooking and browning.
- Drizzle the Thai sweet chili sauce over the meatballs towards the end of cooking for a nice glaze.

Per Serving: Calories: 550; Cholesterol: 205mg; Total Fat: 32g; Saturated Fat: 11g; Sodium: 1300mg; Total Carbohydrates: 36g; Dietary Fiber: 2g; Total Sugars: 23g; Protein: 29g

Eggplant Parmesan Subs

Servings: 2 | Prep Time: 10 Minutes | Cooking Time: 13 Minutes

Ingredients:

- 4 Peeled eggplant slices (about 1.25 cm thick and 7.5 cm in diameter)
- Olive oil spray
- 2 tablespoons plus 2 teaspoons Jarred pizza sauce, any variety except creamy
- ¼ cup (about 20 grams) Finely grated Parmesan cheese
- 2 Small, long soft rolls, such as hero, hoagie,

or Italian sub rolls (gluten-free, if a concern), split open lengthwise

Directions:

1. Preheat the air fryer to 175°C/350°F.
2. When the machine is at temperature, coat both sides of the eggplant slices with olive oil spray. Set them in the basket in one layer and air-fry undisturbed for 10 minutes, until lightly browned and softened.
3. Increase the machine's temperature to 190°C/375°F (or 185°C/370°F, if that's the closest setting—unless the machine is already at 180°C/360°F, in which case leave it alone). Top each eggplant slice with 2 teaspoons pizza sauce, then 1 tablespoon of cheese. Air-fry undisturbed for 2 minutes, or until the cheese has melted.
4. Use a nonstick-safe spatula, and perhaps a flatware fork for balance, to transfer the eggplant slices cheese side up to a cutting board. Set the roll(s) cut side down in the basket in one layer (working in batches as necessary) and air-fry undisturbed for 1 minute, to toast the rolls a bit and warm them up. Set 2 eggplant slices in each warm roll.

Variations & Ingredients Tips:

- Use zucchini slices instead of eggplant for a different vegetable option.
- Add a slice of fresh mozzarella on top of the Parmesan for extra cheesiness.
- Sprinkle some dried herbs like oregano or basil on the eggplant before cooking for extra flavor.

Per Serving (1 sandwich): Calories: 280; Cholesterol: 10mg; Total Fat: 9g; Saturated Fat: 3g; Sodium: 840mg; Total Carbohydrates: 40g; Dietary Fiber: 5g; Total Sugars: 8g; Protein: 11g

Provolone Stuffed Meatballs

Servings: 4 | Prep Time: 20 Minutes | Cooking Time: 12 Minutes

Ingredients:

- 1 tablespoon olive oil
- 1 small onion, very finely chopped
- 1 to 2 cloves garlic, minced
- 340 grams ground beef
- 340 grams ground pork
- ¾ cup breadcrumbs
- ¼ cup grated Parmesan cheese
- ¼ cup finely chopped fresh parsley (or 1 tablespoon dried parsley)
- ½ teaspoon dried oregano
- 1½ teaspoons salt
- freshly ground black pepper
- 2 eggs, lightly beaten
- 140 grams sharp or aged provolone cheese, cut into 2.5-cm cubes

Directions:

1. Preheat a skillet over medium-high heat. Add the oil and cook the onion and garlic until tender, but not browned.
2. Transfer the onion and garlic to a large bowl and add the beef, pork, breadcrumbs, Parmesan cheese, parsley, oregano, salt, pepper and eggs. Mix well until all the ingredients are combined. Divide the mixture into 12 evenly sized balls. Make one meatball at a time, by pressing a hole in the meatball mixture with your finger and pushing a piece of provolone cheese into the hole. Mold the meat back into a ball, enclosing the cheese.
3. Preheat the air fryer to 190°C/380°F.
4. Working in two batches, transfer six of the meatballs to the air fryer basket and air-fry for 12 minutes, shaking the basket and turning the meatballs a couple of times during the cooking process. Repeat with the remaining six meatballs. You can pop the first batch of meatballs into the air fryer for the last two minutes of cooking to re-heat them. Serve warm.

Variations & Ingredients Tips:

- Substitute beef and pork with ground turkey or chicken for a leaner meatball option.
- Use mozzarella or fontina cheese instead of provolone for a milder flavor.
- Serve meatballs with marinara sauce, in sub rolls, or over pasta for a complete meal.

Per Serving (3 meatballs): Calories: 520; Cholesterol: 180mg; Total Fat: 36g; Saturated Fat: 15g; Sodium: 1160mg; Total Carbohydrates: 18g; Dietary Fiber: 1g; Total Sugars: 2g; Protein: 35g

Black Bean Veggie Burgers

Servings: 3 | Prep Time: 15 Minutes | Cooking Time: 10 Minutes

Ingredients:

- 1 cup Drained and rinsed canned black beans
- ⅓ cup Pecan pieces
- ⅓ cup Rolled oats (not quick-cooking or steel-cut; gluten-free, if a concern)
- 2 tablespoons (or 1 small egg) Pasteurized egg substitute, such as Egg Beaters (glu-

- ten-free, if a concern)
- 2 teaspoons Red ketchup-like chili sauce, such as Heinz
- ¼ teaspoon Ground cumin
- ¼ teaspoon Dried oregano
- ¼ teaspoon Table salt
- ¼ teaspoon Ground black pepper
- Olive oil
- Olive oil spray

Directions:

1. Preheat the air fryer to 200°C/400°F.
2. Put the beans, pecans, oats, egg substitute or egg, chili sauce, cumin, oregano, salt, and pepper in a food processor. Cover and process to a coarse paste that will hold its shape like sugar-cookie dough, adding olive oil in 1-teaspoon increments to get the mixture to blend smoothly. The amount of olive oil is actually dependent on the internal moisture content of the beans and the oats. Figure on about 1 tablespoon (three 1-teaspoon additions) for the smaller batch, with proportional increases for the other batches. A little too much olive oil can't hurt, but a dry paste will fall apart as it cooks and a far-too-wet paste will stick to the basket.
3. Scrape down and remove the blade. Using clean, wet hands, form the paste into two 10 cm patties for the small batch, three 10 cm patties for the medium, or four 10 cm patties for the large batch, setting them one by one on a cutting board. Generously coat both sides of the patties with olive oil spray.
4. Set them in the basket in one layer. Air-fry undisturbed for 10 minutes, or until lightly browned and crisp at the edges.
5. Use a nonstick-safe spatula, and perhaps a flatware fork for balance, to transfer the burgers to a wire rack. Cool for 5 minutes before serving.

Variations & Ingredients Tips:

- Add finely chopped vegetables like bell peppers, onions, or carrots for extra flavor and nutrition.
- Experiment with different spices and herbs, such as smoked paprika, garlic powder, or cilantro.
- For a gluten-free version, ensure all ingredients are certified gluten-free.

Per Serving: Calories: 280; Cholesterol: 0mg; Total Fat: 15g; Saturated Fat: 2g; Sodium: 420mg; Total Carbohydrates: 28g; Dietary Fiber: 8g; Total Sugars: 2g; Protein: 10g

Salmon Burgers

Servings: 3 | Prep Time: 15 Minutes | Cooking Time: 8 Minutes

Ingredients:

- 510 grams Skinless salmon fillet, preferably fattier Atlantic salmon
- 1½ tablespoons Minced chives or the green part of a scallion
- ½ cup Plain panko bread crumbs (gluten-free, if a concern)
- 1½ teaspoons Dijon mustard (gluten-free, if a concern)
- 1½ teaspoons Drained and rinsed capers, minced
- 1½ teaspoons Lemon juice
- ¼ teaspoon Table salt
- ¼ teaspoon Ground black pepper
- Vegetable oil spray

Directions:

1. Preheat the air fryer to 190°C/375°F.
2. Cut the salmon into pieces that will fit in a food processor. Cover and pulse until coarsely chopped. Add the chives and pulse to combine, until the fish is ground but not a paste. Scrape down and remove the blade. Scrape the salmon mixture into a bowl. Add the bread crumbs, mustard, capers, lemon juice, salt, and pepper. Stir gently until well combined.
3. Use clean and dry hands to form the mixture into two 12.5-cm patties for a small batch, three 12.5-cm patties for a medium batch, or four 12.5-cm patties for a large one.
4. Coat both sides of each patty with vegetable oil spray. Set them in the basket in one layer and air-fry undisturbed for 8 minutes, or until browned and an instant-read meat thermometer inserted into the center of a burger registers 65°C/145°F.
5. Use a nonstick-safe spatula, and perhaps a flatware fork for balance, to transfer the burgers to a wire rack. Cool for 2 or 3 minutes before serving.

Variations & Ingredients Tips:

- Substitute salmon with canned or leftover cooked salmon for convenience.
- Add finely chopped red bell pepper or celery to the burger mixture for extra crunch and flavor.
- Serve on toasted buns with lettuce, tomato, and a dollop of tartar sauce or remoulade.

Per Serving (1 burger): Calories: 320; Cholesterol: 95mg; Total Fat: 16g; Saturated Fat: 3g; Sodium: 440mg; Total Carbohydrates: 15g; Dietary Fiber: 1g; Total Sugars: 1g; Protein: 31g

Chili Cheese Dogs

Servings: 3 | Prep Time: 10 Minutes | Cooking Time: 12 Minutes

Ingredients:

- 340 grams Lean ground beef
- 1½ tablespoons Chile powder
- 240 grams plus 2 tablespoons Jarred sofrito
- 3 Hot dogs (gluten-free, if a concern)
- 3 Hot dog buns (gluten-free, if a concern), split open lengthwise
- 3 tablespoons Finely chopped scallion
- 60 grams Shredded Cheddar cheese

Directions:

1. Crumble the ground beef into a medium or large saucepan set over medium heat. Brown well, stirring often to break up the clumps. Add the chile powder and cook for 30 seconds, stirring the whole time. Stir in the sofrito and bring to a simmer. Reduce the heat to low and simmer, stirring occasionally, for 5 minutes. Keep warm.
2. Preheat the air fryer to 200°C/400°F.
3. When the machine is at temperature, put the hot dogs in the basket and air-fry undisturbed for 10 minutes, or until the hot dogs are bubbling and blistered, even a little crisp.
4. Use kitchen tongs to put the hot dogs in the buns. Top each with about 120 grams of the ground beef mixture, 1 tablespoon of the minced scallion, and 20 grams of the cheese. (The scallion should go under the cheese so it superheats and wilts a bit.) Set the filled hot dog buns in the basket and air-fry undisturbed for 2 minutes, or until the cheese has melted.
5. Remove the basket from the machine. Cool the chili cheese dogs in the basket for 5 minutes before serving.

Variations & Ingredients Tips:

- Use turkey or veggie hot dogs for a healthier option.
- Substitute cheddar cheese with your favorite melty cheese, such as pepper jack or Swiss.
- Add diced onions or jalapeños to the chili for extra flavor and heat.

Per Serving: Calories: 580; Cholesterol: 110mg; Total Fat: 32g; Saturated Fat: 13g; Sodium: 1420mg; Total Carbohydrates: 36g; Dietary Fiber: 5g; Total Sugars: 6g; Protein: 38g

Chicken Gyros

Servings: 4 | Prep Time: 10 Minutes (plus Marinating Time) | Cooking Time: 14 Minutes

Ingredients:

- 4 110to 140-gram boneless skinless chicken thighs, trimmed of any fat blobs
- 2 tablespoons Lemon juice
- 2 tablespoons Red wine vinegar
- 2 tablespoons Olive oil
- 2 teaspoons Dried oregano
- 2 teaspoons Minced garlic
- 1 teaspoon Table salt
- 1 teaspoon Ground black pepper
- 4 Pita pockets (gluten-free, if a concern)
- ½ cup Chopped tomatoes
- ½ cup Bottled regular, low-fat, or fat-free ranch dressing (gluten-free, if a concern)

Directions:

1. Mix the thighs, lemon juice, vinegar, oil, oregano, garlic, salt, and pepper in a zip-closed bag. Seal, gently massage the marinade into the meat through the plastic, and refrigerate for at least 2 hours or up to 6 hours. (Longer than that and the meat can turn rubbery.)
2. Set the plastic bag out on the counter (to make the contents a little less frigid). Preheat the air fryer to 190°C/375°F.
3. When the machine is at temperature, use kitchen tongs to place the thighs in the basket in one layer. Discard the marinade. Air-fry the chicken thighs undisturbed for 12 minutes, or until browned and an instant-read meat thermometer inserted into the thickest part of one thigh registers 75°C/165°F. You may need to air-fry the chicken 2 minutes longer if the machine's temperature is 70°C/360°F.
4. Use kitchen tongs to transfer the thighs to a cutting board. Cool for 5 minutes, then set one thigh in each of the pita pockets. Top each with 2 tablespoons chopped tomatoes and 2 tablespoons dressing. Serve warm.

Variations & Ingredients Tips:

- Substitute chicken thighs with chicken breast for a leaner option.
- Add shredded lettuce, sliced onions, or cucumbers for extra crunch and flavor.
- Use homemade tzatziki sauce instead of ranch dressing for a more authentic taste.

Per Serving: Calories: 460; Cholesterol: 95mg; Total Fat: 28g; Saturated Fat: 5g; Sodium: 1070mg; Total Carbohydrates: 29g; Dietary Fiber: 2g; Total Sugars: 4g; Protein: 25g

Desserts And Sweets

Carrot Cake With Cream Cheese Icing

Servings: 6 | Prep Time: 30 Minutes | Cooking Time: 55 Minutes

Ingredients:

- 1¼ cups all-purpose flour
- 1 teaspoon baking powder
- ½ teaspoon baking soda
- 1 teaspoon ground cinnamon
- ¼ teaspoon ground nutmeg
- ¼ teaspoon salt
- 2 cups grated carrot (about 3 to 4 medium carrots or 2 large)
- ¾ cup granulated sugar
- ¼ cup brown sugar
- 2 eggs
- ¾ cup canola or vegetable oil
- For the icing:
- 227 grams cream cheese, softened at room temperature
- 113 grams butter (110-g or 1 stick), softened at room temperature
- 1 cup powdered sugar
- 1 teaspoon pure vanilla extract

Directions:

1. Grease a 18-cm cake pan.
2. Combine the flour, baking powder, baking soda, cinnamon, nutmeg and salt in a bowl. Add the grated carrots and toss well.
3. In a separate bowl, beat the sugars and eggs together until light and frothy. Drizzle in the oil, beating constantly. Fold the egg mixture into the dry ingredients until everything is just combined and you no longer see any traces of flour.
4. Pour the batter into the cake pan and wrap the pan completely in greased aluminum foil.
5. Preheat the air fryer to 180°C/350°F.
6. Lower the cake pan into the air fryer basket using a sling made of aluminum foil (fold a piece of aluminum foil into a strip about 5-cm wide by 60-cm long). Fold the ends of the aluminum foil into the air fryer, letting them rest on top of the cake. Air-fry for 40 minutes. Remove the aluminum foil cover and air-fry for an additional 15 minutes or until a skewer inserted into the center of the cake comes out clean and the top is nicely browned.
7. While the cake is cooking, beat the cream cheese, butter, powdered sugar and vanilla extract together using a hand mixer, stand mixer or food processor (or a lot of elbow grease!).
8. Remove the cake pan from the air fryer and let the cake cool in the cake pan for 10 minutes or so. Then remove the cake from the pan and let it continue to cool completely.
9. Frost the cake with the cream cheese icing and serve.

Variations & Ingredients Tips:

- ▶ Add ½ cup of raisins, chopped walnuts, or pecans to the batter.
- ▶ Substitute ¼ cup of the oil with unsweetened applesauce for a lower fat version.
- ▶ Use a lemon cream cheese frosting for a tangy twist.

Per Serving: Calories: 740; Total Fat: 49g; Saturated Fat: 20g; Sodium: 470mg; Total Carbohydrates: 71g; Dietary Fiber: 2g; Total Sugars: 49g; Protein: 8g

Vanilla-strawberry Muffins

Servings: 4 | Prep Time: 10 Minutes | Cooking Time: 25 Minutes

Ingredients:

- 1/4 cup diced strawberries
- 2 tbsp powdered sugar
- 1 cup flour
- 1/2 tsp baking soda
- 1/3 cup granulated sugar
- 1/4 tsp salt
- 1 tsp vanilla extract
- 1 egg
- 1 tbsp butter, melted
- 1/2 cup diced strawberries
- 2 tbsp chopped walnuts

- 6 tbsp butter, softened
- 1 1/2 cups powdered sugar
- 1/8 tsp peppermint extract

Directions:

1. Preheat air fryer at 190°C/375°F.
2. Combine flour, baking soda, granulated sugar, and salt in a bowl.
3. In another bowl, combine the vanilla, egg, walnuts and melted butter.
4. Pour wet ingredients into dry ingredients and toss to combine.
5. Fold in half of the strawberries and spoon mixture into 8 greased silicone cupcake liners.
6. Place cupcakes in the frying basket and Bake for 6-8 minutes.
7. Let cool onto a cooling rack for 10 minutes.
8. Blend the remaining strawberries in a food processor until smooth.
9. Slowly add powdered sugar to softened butter while beating in a bowl. Stir in peppermint extract and puréed strawberries until blended.
10. Spread over cooled cupcakes. Serve sprinkled with powdered sugar.

Variations & Ingredients Tips:

- Use other berries like raspberries or blueberries instead of strawberries.
- Add lemon or orange zest to the batter.
- Top with cream cheese frosting instead of strawberry buttercream.

Per Serving (2 muffins): Calories: 510; Total Fat: 18g; Saturated Fat: 9g; Cholesterol: 70mg; Sodium: 280mg; Total Carbs: 83g; Dietary Fiber: 2g; Total Sugars: 57g; Protein: 5g

Roasted Pears

Servings: 4 | Prep Time: 5 Minutes | Cooking Time: 10 Minutes

Ingredients:

- 2 Ripe pears, preferably Anjou, stemmed, peeled, halved lengthwise, and cored
- 2 tablespoons Butter, melted
- 2 teaspoons Granulated white sugar
- Grated nutmeg
- 1/4 cup Honey
- 1/2 cup (about 30g) Shaved Parmesan cheese

Directions:

1. Preheat the air fryer to 200°C/400°F.
2. Brush each pear half with about 5ml of the melted butter, then sprinkle their cut sides with 1/2 teaspoon sugar. Grate a pinch of nutmeg over each pear.
3. When the machine is at temperature, set the pear halves cut side up in the basket with as much air space between them as possible. Air-fry undisturbed for 10 minutes, or until hot and softened.
4. Use a nonstick-safe spatula, and perhaps a flatware tablespoon for balance, to transfer the pear halves to a serving platter or plates. Cool for a minute or two, then drizzle each pear half with 1 tablespoon of the honey. Lay about 2 tablespoons of shaved Parmesan over each half just before serving.

Variations & Ingredients Tips:

- Use maple syrup instead of honey.
- Sprinkle with cinnamon instead of nutmeg.
- Top with chopped toasted nuts like almonds or pecans.

Per Serving: Calories: 190; Total Fat: 9g; Saturated Fat: 5g; Cholesterol: 20mg; Sodium: 130mg; Total Carbs: 27g; Dietary Fiber: 3g; Total Sugars: 21g; Protein: 3g

Nutella® Torte

Servings: 6 | Prep Time: 15 Minutes | Cooking Time: 55 Minutes

Ingredients:

- 1/4 cup unsalted butter, softened
- 1/2 cup sugar
- 2 eggs
- 1 teaspoon vanilla
- 1 1/4 cups Nutella® (or other chocolate hazelnut spread), divided
- 1/4 cup flour
- 1 teaspoon baking powder
- 1/4 teaspoon salt
- Dark chocolate fudge topping
- Coarsely chopped toasted hazelnuts

Directions:

1. Cream the butter and sugar together with an electric hand mixer until light and fluffy. Add the eggs, vanilla, and 3/4 cup of the Nutella® and mix until combined. Combine the flour, baking powder and salt together, and add these dry ingredients to the butter mixture, beating for 1 minute.
2. Preheat the air fryer to 180°C/350°F.
3. Grease a 18-cm cake pan with butter and then line the bottom of the pan with a circle of parchment paper. Grease the parchment paper circle as well. Pour the

batter into the prepared cake pan and wrap the pan completely with aluminum foil. Lower the pan into the air fryer basket with an aluminum sling (fold a piece of aluminum foil into a strip about 5-cm wide by 60-cm long). Fold the ends of the aluminum foil over the top of the dish before returning the basket to the air fryer. Air-fry for 30 minutes. Remove the foil and air-fry for another 25 minutes.
4. Remove the cake from air fryer and let it cool for 10 minutes. Invert the cake onto a plate, remove the parchment paper and invert the cake back onto a serving platter. While the cake is still warm, spread the remaining 1/2 cup of Nutella® over the top of the cake. Melt the dark chocolate fudge in the microwave for about 10 seconds so it melts enough to be pourable. Drizzle the sauce on top of the cake in a zigzag motion. Turn the cake 90 degrees and drizzle more sauce in zigzags perpendicular to the first zigzags. Garnish the edges of the torte with the toasted hazelnuts and serve.

Variations & Ingredients Tips:

- Substitute other nut butters like almond or peanut butter for some of the Nutella.
- Top with fresh berries in addition to the hazelnuts.
- Dust with powdered sugar before serving.

Per Serving: Calories: 525; Total Fat: 30g; Saturated Fat: 11g; Cholesterol: 90mg; Sodium: 160mg; Total Carbs: 59g; Dietary Fiber: 2g; Total Sugars: 40g; Protein: 8g

Fall Caramelized Apples

Servings: 2 | Prep Time: 5 Minutes | Cooking Time: 25 Minutes

Ingredients:

- 2 apples, sliced
- 1 ½ tsp brown sugar
- ¼ tsp cinnamon
- ¼ tsp nutmeg
- ¼ tsp salt
- 1 tsp lemon zest

Directions:

1. Preheat air fryer to 200°C/390°F.
2. Set the apples upright in a baking pan. Add 2 tbsp of water to the bottom to keep the apples moist.
3. Sprinkle the tops with sugar, lemon zest, cinnamon, and nutmeg. Lightly sprinkle the halves with salt and the tops with oil.
4. Bake for 20 minutes or until the apples are tender and golden on top.
5. Enjoy.

Variations & Ingredients Tips:

- Use pears, peaches, or plums instead of apples.
- Add a scoop of vanilla ice cream or a dollop of whipped cream on top.
- Sprinkle with granola or chopped nuts for extra crunch.

Per Serving: Calories: 120; Total Fat: 0g; Saturated Fat: 0g; Sodium: 300mg; Total Carbohydrates: 32g; Dietary Fiber: 5g; Total Sugars: 25g; Protein: 0g

Chocolate Cake

Servings: 8 | Prep Time: 10 Minutes | Cooking Time: 20 Minutes

Ingredients:

- 1/2 cup sugar
- 1/4 cup flour, plus 3 tablespoons
- 3 tablespoons cocoa
- 1/2 teaspoon baking powder
- 1/2 teaspoon baking soda
- 1/4 teaspoon salt
- 1 egg
- 2 tablespoons oil
- 1/2 cup milk
- 1/2 teaspoon vanilla extract

Directions:

1. Preheat air fryer to 165°C/330°F.
2. Grease and flour a 15x15cm baking pan.
3. In a bowl, stir together sugar, flours, cocoa, baking powder, soda and salt.
4. Add egg, oil, milk and vanilla. Beat with a whisk until smooth.
5. Pour batter into prepared pan.
6. Bake at 330°F for 20 minutes until toothpick inserted comes out clean.

Variations & Ingredients Tips:

- Add chocolate chips or chopped nuts to the batter.
- Substitute buttermilk for a moister cake.
- Top with chocolate frosting or powdered sugar.

Per Serving: Calories: 149; Total Fat: 4g; Saturated Fat: 1g; Sodium: 158mg; Total Carbohydrates: 26g; Dietary Fiber: 1g; Total Sugars: 14g; Protein: 3g

Cheese & Honey Stuffed Figs

Servings: 4 | Prep Time: 10 Minutes | Cooking Time: 15 Minutes

Ingredients:

- 8 figs, stem off
- 57 grams cottage cheese
- ¼ tsp ground cinnamon
- ¼ tsp orange zest
- ¼ tsp vanilla extract
- 2 tbsp honey
- 1 tbsp olive oil

Directions:

1. Preheat air fryer to 180°C/360°F.
2. Cut an "X" in the top of each fig 1/3 way through, leaving intact the base.
3. Mix together the cottage cheese, cinnamon, orange zest, vanilla extract and 1 tbsp of honey in a bowl.
4. Spoon the cheese mixture into the cavity of each fig.
5. Put the figs in a single layer in the air fryer basket. Drizzle the olive oil over the top of the figs and Roast for 10 minutes.
6. Drizzle with the remaining honey. Serve and enjoy!

Variations & Ingredients Tips:

- Use ricotta, mascarpone, or goat cheese instead of cottage cheese.
- Substitute figs with pitted dates or apricots.
- Sprinkle with chopped pistachios or walnuts before serving.

Per Serving: Calories: 180; Total Fat: 6g; Saturated Fat: 1.5g; Sodium: 85mg; Total Carbohydrates: 30g; Dietary Fiber: 3g; Total Sugars: 26g; Protein: 4g

Dark Chokolate Cookies

Servings: 4 | Prep Time: 20 Minutes | Cooking Time: 50 Minutes

Ingredients:

- 1/3 cup brown sugar
- 2 tbsp butter, softened
- 1 egg yolk
- 2/3 cup flour
- 5 tbsp peanut butter
- ¼ tsp baking soda
- 1 tsp dark rum
- ½ cup dark chocolate chips

Directions:

1. Preheat air fryer to 155°C/310°F.
2. Beat butter and brown sugar in a bowl until fluffy. Stir in the egg yolk.
3. Add flour, 3 tbsp of peanut butter, baking soda, and rum until well mixed.
4. Spread the batter into a parchment-lined baking pan. Bake in the air fryer until the cooking is lightly brown and just set, 7-10 minutes.
5. Remove from the fryer and let cool for 10 minutes.
6. After, remove the cookie from the pan and the parchment paper and cool on the wire rack.
7. When cooled, combine the chips with the remaining peanut butter in a heatproof cup. Place in the air fryer and Bake until melted, 2 minutes. Remove and stir.
8. Spread on the cooled cookies and serve.

Variations & Ingredients Tips:

- Use milk chocolate or white chocolate chips for a sweeter cookie.
- Substitute dark rum with vanilla extract for an alcohol-free version.
- Add chopped nuts like almonds or hazelnuts to the batter.

Per Serving: Calories: 430; Total Fat: 24g; Saturated Fat: 9g; Sodium: 260mg; Total Carbohydrates: 51g; Dietary Fiber: 3g; Total Sugars: 30g; Protein: 8g

Choco-granola Bars With Cranberries

Servings: 6 | Prep Time: 10 Minutes | Cooking Time: 20 Minutes

Ingredients:

- 2 tbsp dark chocolate chunks
- 2 cups quick oats
- 2 tbsp dried cranberries
- 3 tbsp shredded coconut
- 1/2 cup maple syrup
- 1 tsp ground cinnamon
- 1/8 tsp salt
- 2 tbsp smooth peanut butter

Directions:

1. Preheat air fryer to 180°C/360°F.
2. Stir together all ingredients in a bowl until well combined.
3. Press oat mixture into a parchment-lined baking pan in a single layer.
4. Place pan in air fryer basket and bake for 15 minutes.

5. Remove pan and lift granola out using parchment edges.
6. Let cool 5 minutes, then slice and serve.

Variations & Ingredients Tips:

▶ Use different dried fruits like raisins or chopped apricots.
▶ Substitute almond or cashew butter for peanut butter.
▶ Drizzle with melted chocolate after baking.

Per Serving: Calories: 238; Total Fat: 8g; Saturated Fat: 4g; Sodium: 78mg; Total Carbohydrates: 36g; Dietary Fiber: 4g; Total Sugars: 16g; Protein: 5g

Sweet Potato Pie Rolls

Servings: 3 | Prep Time: 15 Minutes | Cooking Time: 8 Minutes

Ingredients:

- 6 Spring roll wrappers
- 1½ cups Canned yams in syrup, drained
- 2 tablespoons Light brown sugar
- 1/4 teaspoon Ground cinnamon
- 1 Large egg, well beaten
- Vegetable oil spray

Directions:

1. Preheat the air fryer to 200°C/400°F.
2. Set a spring roll wrapper on a clean, dry work surface. Scoop up 1/4 cup of the pulpy yams and set along one edge of the wrapper, leaving 5cm on each side of the yams.
3. Top the yams with about 1 teaspoon brown sugar and a pinch of ground cinnamon.
4. Fold the sides of the wrapper perpendicular to the yam filling up and over the filling, partially covering it. Brush beaten egg over the side of the wrapper farthest from the yam.
5. Starting with the yam end, roll the wrapper closed, ending at the part with the beaten egg that you can press gently to seal. Lightly coat the roll on all sides with vegetable oil spray.
6. Set it aside seam side down and continue filling, rolling, and spraying the remaining wrappers in the same way.
7. Set the rolls seam side down in the basket with as much air space between them as possible. Air-fry undisturbed for 8 minutes, or until crisp and golden brown.
8. Use a nonstick-safe spatula and perhaps kitchen tongs for balance to gently transfer the rolls to a wire rack. Cool for at least 5 minutes or up to 30 minutes before serving.

Variations & Ingredients Tips:

▶ Use fresh baked sweet potatoes instead of canned.
▶ Add pecans or walnuts to the filling.
▶ Drizzle with maple syrup before serving.

Per Serving: Calories: 275; Total Fat: 3g; Saturated Fat: 0.5g; Cholesterol: 50mg; Sodium: 240mg; Total Carbs: 58g; Dietary Fiber: 4g; Total Sugars: 24g; Protein: 4g

Dark Chocolate Cream Galette

Servings: 4 | Prep Time: 15 Minutes | Cooking Time: 55 Minutes + Cooling Time

Ingredients:

- 454 grams cream cheese, softened
- 1 cup crumbled graham crackers
- 1 cup dark cocoa powder
- ½ cup white sugar
- 1 tsp peppermint extract
- 1 tsp ground cinnamon
- 1 egg
- 1 cup condensed milk
- 2 tbsp muscovado sugar
- 1 ½ tsp butter, melted

Directions:

1. Preheat air fryer to 180°C/350°F.
2. Place the crumbled graham crackers in a large bowl and stir in the muscovado sugar and melted butter. Spread the mixture into a greased pie pan, pressing down to form the galette base.
3. Place the pan into the air fryer and Bake for 5 minutes. Remove the pan and set aside.
4. Place the cocoa powder, cream cheese, peppermint extract, white sugar, cinnamon, condensed milk, and egg in a large bowl and whip thoroughly to combine.
5. Spoon the chocolate mixture over the graham cracker crust and level the top with a spatula. Put in the air fryer and Bake for 40 minutes until firm.
6. Transfer the galette to a wire rack to cool. Serve and enjoy!

Variations & Ingredients Tips:

▶ Use milk chocolate or white chocolate instead of dark for a sweeter flavor.
▶ Add espresso powder or instant coffee to the filling for a mocha twist.
▶ Top with fresh berries, whipped cream, or a dusting of powdered sugar.

Per Serving: Calories: 780; Total Fat: 50g; Saturated Fat: 29g; Sodium: 510mg; Total Carbohydrates: 77g; Dietary Fiber: 5g; Total Sugars: 61g; Protein: 15g

Air-fried Strawberry Hand Tarts

Servings: 9 | Prep Time: 45 Minutes | Cooking Time: 9 Minutes

Ingredients:

- ½ cup butter, softened
- ½ cup sugar
- 2 eggs
- 1 teaspoon vanilla extract
- 2 tablespoons lemon zest
- 2½ cups all-purpose flour
- 1 teaspoon baking powder
- ¼ teaspoon salt
- 1¼ cups strawberry jam, divided
- 1 egg white, beaten
- 1 cup powdered sugar
- 2 teaspoons milk

Directions:

1. Combine the butter and sugar in a bowl and beat with an electric mixer until the mixture is light and fluffy. Add the eggs one at a time. Add the vanilla extract and lemon zest and mix well.
2. In a separate bowl, combine the flour, baking powder and salt. Add the dry ingredients to the wet ingredients, mixing just until the dough comes together.
3. Transfer the dough to a floured surface and knead by hand for 10 minutes. Cover with a clean kitchen towel and let the dough rest for 30 minutes. (Alternatively, dough can be mixed and kneaded in a stand mixer.)
4. Divide the dough in half and roll each half out into a 0.6-cm thick rectangle that measures 30-cm x 23-cm. Cut each rectangle of dough into nine 10-cm x 7.5-cm rectangles (a pizza cutter is very helpful for this task). You should have 18 rectangles.
5. Spread two teaspoons of strawberry jam in the center of nine of the rectangles leaving a 0.6-cm border around the edges. Brush the egg white around the edges of each rectangle and top with the remaining nine rectangles of dough. Press the back of a fork around the edges to seal the tarts shut. Brush the top of the tarts with the beaten egg white and pierce the dough three or four times down the center of the tart with a fork.
6. Preheat the air fryer to 180°C/350°F.
7. Air-fry the tarts in batches at 180°C/350°F for 6 minutes. Flip the tarts over and air-fry for an additional 3 minutes.
8. While the tarts are air-frying, make the icing. Combine the powdered sugar, ¼ cup strawberry preserves and milk in a bowl, whisking until the icing is smooth.
9. Spread the icing over the top of each tart, leaving an empty border around the edges. Decorate with sprinkles if desired.

Variations & Ingredients Tips:

- Substitute strawberry jam with raspberry, blueberry, or apricot preserves.
- Add a pinch of ground cinnamon or nutmeg to the dough for extra flavor.
- Drizzle with melted white or dark chocolate instead of icing.

Per Serving: Calories: 410; Total Fat: 14g; Saturated Fat: 8g; Sodium: 200mg; Total Carbohydrates: 68g; Dietary Fiber: 1g; Total Sugars: 40g; Protein: 5g

Donut Holes

Servings: 13 | Prep Time: 15 Minutes | Cooking Time: 12 Minutes

Ingredients:

- 6 tablespoons Granulated white sugar
- 1½ tablespoons Butter, melted and cooled
- 2 tablespoons (or 1 small egg, well beaten) Pasteurized egg substitute, such as Egg Beaters
- 6 tablespoons Regular or low-fat sour cream (not fat-free)
- ¾ teaspoon Vanilla extract
- 1⅔ cups All-purpose flour
- ¾ teaspoon Baking powder
- ¼ teaspoon Table salt
- Vegetable oil spray

Directions:

1. Preheat the air fryer to 180°C/350°F.
2. Whisk the sugar and melted butter in a medium bowl until well combined. Whisk in the egg substitute or egg, then the sour cream and vanilla until smooth. Remove the whisk and stir in the flour, baking powder, and salt with a wooden spoon just until a soft dough forms.
3. Use 2 tablespoons of this dough to create a ball between your clean palms. Set it aside and continue making balls: 8 more for the small batch, 12 more for the medium batch, or 17 more for the large one.
4. Coat the balls in the vegetable oil spray, then set them in the basket with as much air space between them as possible. Even a fraction of 0.25 cm will be enough, but they should not touch. Air-fry undisturbed for 12 minutes, or until browned and cooked through. A tooth-

pick inserted into the center of a ball should come out clean.
5. Pour the contents of the basket onto a wire rack. Cool for at least 5 minutes before serving.

Variations & Ingredients Tips:

▶ Toss the warm donut holes in cinnamon sugar or powdered sugar.
▶ Add grated lemon or orange zest to the batter for a citrusy flavor.
▶ Fill the donut holes with jam, Nutella, or pastry cream using a piping bag.

Per Serving: Calories: 130; Total Fat: 5g; Saturated Fat: 3g; Sodium: 100mg; Total Carbohydrates: 20g; Dietary Fiber: 0g; Total Sugars: 9g; Protein: 2g

Mom's Amaretto Cheesecake

Servings: 6 | Prep Time: 20 Minutes | Cooking Time: 35 Minutes

Ingredients:

- 2/3 cup slivered almonds
- 1/2 cup Corn Chex
- 1 tbsp light brown sugar
- 3 tbsp butter, melted
- 400g cream cheese
- 2 tbsp sour cream
- 1/2 cup granulated sugar
- 1/2 cup Amaretto liqueur
- 1/2 tsp lemon juice
- 2 tbsp almond flakes

Directions:

1. In a food processor, pulse corn Chex, almonds, and brown sugar until it has a powdered consistency. Transfer it to a bowl. Stir in melted butter with a fork until butter is well distributed. Press mixture into a greased 20cm cake pan.
2. Preheat air fryer to 200°C/400°F.
3. In a bowl, combine cream cheese, sour cream, granulated sugar, Amaretto liqueur, and lemon juice until smooth. Pour it over the crust and cover with aluminum foil.
4. Place springform pan in the air fryer basket and bake for 16 minutes. Remove the foil and cook for 6 more minutes until a little jiggly in the center.
5. Let sit covered in the fridge for at least 2 hours. Release side of pan and serve sprinkled with almond flakes.

Variations & Ingredients Tips:

▶ Use vanilla wafers or graham crackers instead of Corn Chex for the crust.
▶ Substitute Amaretto with 5ml almond extract for a non-alcoholic version.
▶ Top with fresh berries or a drizzle of chocolate sauce before serving.

Per Serving: Calories: 520; Total Fat: 38g; Saturated Fat: 20g; Cholesterol: 100mg; Sodium: 310mg; Total Carbs: 32g; Dietary Fiber: 2g; Total Sugars: 25g; Protein: 9g

Giant Buttery Oatmeal Cookie

Servings: 4 | Prep Time: 15 Minutes | Cooking Time: 16 Minutes

Ingredients:

- 1 cup Rolled oats (not quick-cooking or steel-cut oats)
- ½ cup All-purpose flour
- ½ teaspoon Baking soda
- ½ teaspoon Ground cinnamon
- ½ teaspoon Table salt
- 3½ tablespoons Butter, at room temperature
- ⅓ cup Packed dark brown sugar
- 1½ tablespoons Granulated white sugar
- 3 tablespoons (or 1 medium egg, well beaten) Pasteurized egg substitute, such as Egg Beaters
- ¾ teaspoon Vanilla extract
- ⅓ cup Chopped pecans
- Baking spray

Directions:

1. Preheat the air fryer to 180°C/350°F.
2. Stir the oats, flour, baking soda, cinnamon, and salt in a bowl until well combined.
3. Using an electric hand mixer at medium speed, beat the butter, brown sugar, and granulated white sugar until creamy and thick, about 3 minutes, scraping down the inside of the bowl occasionally. Beat in the egg substitute or egg (as applicable) and vanilla until uniform.
4. Scrape down and remove the beaters. Fold in the flour mixture and pecans with a rubber spatula just until all the flour is moistened and the nuts are even throughout the dough.
5. For a small air fryer, coat the inside of a 15-cm round cake pan with baking spray. For a medium air fryer, coat the inside of an 18-cm round cake pan with baking spray. And for a large air fryer, coat the inside of a 20-cm round cake pan with baking spray. Scrape and gently press the dough into the prepared pan, spreading it into an even layer to the perimeter.

6. Set the pan in the basket and air-fry undisturbed for 16 minutes, or until puffed and browned.
7. Transfer the pan to a wire rack and cool for 10 minutes. Loosen the cookie from the perimeter with a spatula, then invert the pan onto a cutting board and let the cookie come free. Remove the pan and reinvert the cookie onto the wire rack. Cool for 5 minutes more before slicing into wedges to serve.

Variations & Ingredients Tips:

- Use quick oats or old-fashioned oats for a chewier texture.
- Add ½ cup of raisins, dried cranberries, or chocolate chips to the dough.
- Sprinkle with a mixture of cinnamon and sugar before baking for extra flavor.

Per Serving: Calories: 430; Total Fat: 22g; Saturated Fat: 8g; Sodium: 400mg; Total Carbohydrates: 54g; Dietary Fiber: 4g; Total Sugars: 25g; Protein: 7g

Molten Chocolate Almond Cakes

Servings: 3 | Prep Time: 15 Minutes | Cooking Time: 13 Minutes

Ingredients:

- Butter and flour for the ramekins
- 115g bittersweet chocolate, chopped
- 1/2 cup (1 stick) unsalted butter
- 2 eggs
- 2 egg yolks
- 1/4 cup sugar
- 1/2 teaspoon pure vanilla or almond extract
- 1 tablespoon all-purpose flour
- 3 tablespoons ground almonds
- 8 to 12 semisweet chocolate discs (or 4 chunks)
- Cocoa powder or powdered sugar, for dusting
- Toasted almonds, coarsely chopped

Directions:

1. Butter and flour three 170g ramekins.
2. Melt chocolate and butter together.
3. In another bowl, beat eggs, yolks and sugar until light and smooth. Add extract.
4. Whisk chocolate mixture into egg mixture.
5. Stir in flour and ground almonds.
6. Preheat air fryer to 165°C/330°F.
7. Fill ramekins halfway with batter. Add chocolate discs/chunks. Top with remaining batter to 1.3cm from top.
8. Air fry for 13 minutes until sides are set but centers slightly soft.
9. Let sit 5 minutes, then unmold onto plates.
10. Dust with cocoa/powdered sugar. Serve with ice cream and chopped toasted almonds.

Variations & Ingredients Tips:

- Use different nuts like hazelnuts or pistachios.
- Add a splash of liqueur like Frangelico.
- Top with caramel or fruit sauce instead of powdered sugar.

Per Serving: Calories: 570; Total Fat: 41g; Saturated Fat: 20g; Sodium: 85mg; Total Carbohydrates: 46g; Dietary Fiber: 4g; Total Sugars: 34g; Protein: 9g

Vegan Brownie Bites

Servings: 10 | Prep Time: 10 Minutes | Cooking Time: 8 Minutes

Ingredients:

- 2/3 cup walnuts
- 1/3 cup all-purpose flour
- 1/4 cup dark cocoa powder
- 1/3 cup cane sugar
- 1/4 teaspoon salt
- 2 tablespoons vegetable oil
- 1 teaspoon pure vanilla extract
- 1 tablespoon almond milk
- 1 tablespoon powdered sugar

Directions:

1. Preheat the air fryer to 175°C/350°F.
2. To a blender or food processor fitted with a metal blade, add the walnuts, flour, cocoa powder, sugar, and salt. Pulse until smooth, about 30 seconds.
3. Add in the oil, vanilla, and milk and pulse until a dough is formed.
4. Remove the dough and place in a bowl. Form into 10 equal-size bites.
5. Liberally spray the metal trivet in the air fryer basket with olive oil mist. Place the brownie bites into the basket and cook for 8 minutes, or until the outer edges begin to slightly crack.
6. Remove the basket from the air fryer and let cool. Sprinkle the brownie bites with powdered sugar and serve.

Variations & Ingredients Tips:

- Use other nut varieties like pecans or almonds.
- Add chocolate chips or dried fruit to the batter.
- Use oat flour instead of regular flour to make gluten-free.

Per Serving (1 brownie bite): Calories: 110; Total Fat: 7g; Saturated Fat: 1g; Sodium: 50mg; Total Carbs: 12g; Dietary Fiber: 2g; Total Sugars: 6g; Protein: 2g

Rustic Berry Layer Cake

Servings: 6 | Prep Time: 15 Minutes | Cooking Time: 45 Minutes

Ingredients:

- 2 eggs, beaten
- 1/2 cup milk
- 2 tbsp Greek yogurt
- 1/4 cup maple syrup
- 1 tbsp apple cider vinegar
- 1 tbsp vanilla extract
- 3/4 cup all-purpose flour
- 1 tsp baking powder
- 1/2 tsp baking soda
- 1/4 cup dark chocolate chips
- 1/3 cup raspberry jam

Directions:

1. Preheat air fryer to 175°C/350°F.
2. Combine the eggs, milk, Greek yogurt, maple syrup, apple cider vinegar, and vanilla extract in a bowl.
3. Toss in flour, baking powder, and baking soda until combined.
4. Pour the batter into a 15cm round cake pan, distributing well, and Bake for 20-25 minutes until a toothpick comes out clean. Let cool completely.
5. Turn the cake onto a plate, cut lengthwise to make 2 equal layers. Set aside.
6. Add chocolate chips to a heat-proof bowl and Bake for 3 minutes until fully melted.
7. In the meantime, spread raspberry jam on top of the bottom layer, distributing well, and top with the remaining layer.
8. Once the chocolate is ready, stir in 1 tbsp of milk. Pour over the layer cake and spread well.
9. Cut into 6 wedges and serve immediately.

Variations & Ingredients Tips:

- Use other berry jams like strawberry or blueberry.
- Substitute dark chocolate with white or milk chocolate.
- Top with fresh berries and whipped cream.

Per Serving: Calories: 270; Total Fat: 8g; Saturated Fat: 3g; Cholesterol: 60mg; Sodium: 200mg; Total Carbs: 44g; Dietary Fiber: 2g; Total Sugars: 20g; Protein: 6g

Banana Fritters

Servings: 6 | Prep Time: 10 Minutes | Cooking Time: 20 Minutes

Ingredients:

- 1 egg
- 1/4 cup cornstarch
- 1/4 cup bread crumbs
- 3 bananas, halved crosswise
- 1/4 cup caramel sauce

Directions:

1. Preheat air fryer to 175°C/350°F.
2. Set up 3 bowls: cornstarch, beaten egg, bread crumbs.
3. Dip bananas first in cornstarch, then egg, then bread crumbs.
4. Place in greased air fryer basket and spray with oil.
5. Air Fry for 8 minutes, flipping once at 5 minutes.
6. Remove to a plate and drizzle with caramel sauce.
7. Serve warm.

Variations & Ingredients Tips:

- Use panko breadcrumbs for extra crunch.
- Add cinnamon or nutmeg to the breadcrumb mixture.
- Dust with powdered sugar after frying.

Per Serving: Calories: 134; Total Fat: 2g; Saturated Fat: 0g; Sodium: 108mg; Total Carbohydrates: 30g; Dietary Fiber: 2g; Total Sugars: 13g; Protein: 2g

Holiday Peppermint Cake

Servings: 4 | Prep Time: 10 Minutes | Cooking Time: 20 Minutes

Ingredients:

- 1 1/2 cups flour
- 3 eggs
- 1/3 cup molasses
- 1/2 cup olive oil
- 1/2 cup almond milk
- 1/2 tsp vanilla extract
- 1/2 tsp peppermint extract
- 1 tsp baking powder
- 1/2 tsp salt

Directions:

1. Preheat air fryer to 190°C/380°F.

2. Whisk the eggs and molasses until smooth.
3. Slowly mix in olive oil, almond milk, vanilla and peppermint extracts.
4. In another bowl, sift together flour, baking powder and salt.
5. Gradually incorporate dry ingredients into wet ingredients until combined.
6. Pour batter into a greased baking pan and place in air fryer basket.
7. Bake for 12-15 minutes until a toothpick inserted comes out clean.
8. Serve and enjoy!

Variations & Ingredients Tips:

- Use coconut or vegetable oil instead of olive oil.
- Add crushed peppermint candies or chocolate chips to the batter.
- Top with peppermint frosting or whipped cream.

Per Serving: Calories: 538; Total Fat: 27g; Saturated Fat: 4g; Sodium: 307mg; Total Carbohydrates: 67g; Dietary Fiber: 2g; Total Sugars: 28g; Protein: 8g

INDEX

A

Air-fried Strawberry Hand Tarts	88
Almond-crusted Fish	51
Apple Rollups	23
Apple-cinnamon-walnut Muffins	18
Arancini With Sun-dried Tomatoes And Mozzarella	25
Asian Glazed Meatballs	79
Asy Carnitas	43
Avocado Fries With Quick Salsa Fresca	24

B

Bacon-wrapped Asparagus	68
Baked Eggs	17
Balsamic Beef & Veggie Skewers	44
Balsamic Grape Dip	25
Balsamic Marinated Rib Eye Steak With Balsamic Fried Cipollini Onions	41
Banana Fritters	91
Barbecue Chicken Nachos	27
Basic Fried Tofu	56
Basil Feta Crostini	26
Beef Steak Sliders	24
Beer Battered Onion Rings	28
Beer-breaded Halibut Fish Tacos	52
Berbere Beef Steaks	42
Berbere Eggplant Dip	64
Black Bean Veggie Burgers	80
Black Olive & Shrimp Salad	48
Blistered Tomatoes	70
Blooming Onion	20
Blueberry Applesauce Oat Cake	18
Brown Sugar Grapefruit	12
Buttermilk-fried Drumsticks	30
Buttery Chicken Legs	34

C

Cajun Chicken Livers	37
Cajun Pork Loin Chops	46
Cajun-seasoned Shrimp	48
Calf's Liver	45
California Burritos	39
Caponata Salsa	22
Caraway Seed Pretzel Sticks	65

Carrot Cake With Cream Cheese Icing	83
Cheese & Honey Stuffed Figs	86
Cheese Straws	28
Cheeseburger Sliders With Pickle Sauce	38
Cheesy Cauliflower Tart	68
Cheesy Salmon-stuffed Avocados	50
Cheesy Spinach Dip(2)	23
Chicken Adobo	36
Chicken Chunks	34
Chicken Club Sandwiches	78
Chicken Gyros	82
Chicken Saltimbocca Sandwiches	78
Chicken Spiedies	75
Chicken Strips	31
Chili Cheese Dogs	82
Chinese-style Potstickers	22
Choco-granola Bars With Cranberries	86
Chocolate Almond Crescent Rolls	16
Chocolate Cake	85
Christmas Chicken & Roasted Grape Salad	37
Cilantro Sea Bass	54
Citrusy Brussels Sprouts	67
Classic Stuffed Shells	71
Coconut Chicken With Apricot-ginger Sauce	35

Crab Cakes	54
Crispy Duck With Cherry Sauce	36
Crispy Ham And Eggs	40
Crispy Pierogi With Kielbasa And Onions	41
Crispy Samosa Rolls	14
Crunchy Chicken Strips	38
Crunchy Falafel Balls	74
Crunchy Parmesan Edamame	27
Curried Fruit	65

D

Dark Chocolate Cream Galette	87
Dark Chokolate Cookies	86
Delicious Juicy Pork Meatballs	44
Dijon Roasted Purple Potatoes	69
Donut Holes	88

E

Easy Scallops With Lemon Butter	50
Easy Zucchini Lasagna Roll-ups	60
Eggplant Parmesan Subs	79

F

Fall Caramelized Apples	85
Fancy Cranberry Muffins	14
Fiery Bacon-wrapped Dates	21
Fish Nuggets With Broccoli Dip	52
Fish Piccata With Crispy Potatoes	49

French Toast Sticks Recipes 14

Fusion Tender Flank Steak 42

G

Garlic Breadsticks 25

Garlic Wings 21

Garlic-butter Lobster Tails 50

Garlic-parmesan Popcorn 68

Giant Buttery Oatmeal Cookie 89

Greek Street Tacos 29

Green Egg Quiche 19

H

Ham & Cheese Sandwiches 18

Harissa Veggie Fries 58

Hazelnut-crusted Fish 47

Holiday Lobster Salad 51

Holiday Peppermint Cake 91

Honey Lemon Thyme Glazed Cornish Hen 31

Honey Oatmeal 12

Honey Tater Tots With Bacon 22

Honey-mustard Asparagus Puffs 67

Horseradish Mustard Pork Chops 46

I

Indian Chicken Tandoori 33

Indonesian Pork Satay 40

Inside Out Cheeseburgers 77

K

Kale & Rice Chicken Rolls 33

Kentucky-style Pork Tenderloin 45

Kid's Flounder Fingers 53

L

Lamb Burgers 74

M

Masala Fish 'n' Chips 53

Meaty Omelet 12

Mediterranean Granola 17

Mediterranean Salmon Cakes 54

Mexican Cheeseburgers 76

Mini Everything Bagels 13

Molten Chocolate Almond Cakes 90

Mom's Amaretto Cheesecake 89

N

Nutella® Torte 84

O

Okra 69

Orange Trail Oatmeal 15

P

Parmesan Garlic Fries 70

Perfect Burgers 76

Philly Cheesesteak Sandwiches 73

Pickle Brined Fried Chicken 32

Pinto Taquitos	61
Pork Taco Gorditas	39
Prosciutto Chicken Rolls	32
Provolone Stuffed Meatballs	80

Q

Quinoa & Black Bean Stuffed Peppers	59
Quinoa Burgers With Feta Cheese And Dill	56

R

Rainbow Quinoa Patties	62
Ranch Chicken Tortillas	34
Restaurant-style Chicken Thighs	31
Reuben Sandwiches	75
Roasted Pears	84
Roasted Vegetable Stromboli	57
Rustic Berry Layer Cake	91

S

Salmon Burgers	81
Sea Bass With Fruit Salsa	52
Seedy Bagels	13
Sesame Orange Tofu With Snow Peas	59
Shakshuka-style Pepper Cups	15
Shoestring Butternut Squash Fries	66
Sicilian Arancini	66
Smoked Avocado Wedges	65
Smooth & Silky Cauliflower Purée	69
Soft Pretzels	16
Southwest Cornbread	16
Southwest Gluten-free Turkey Meatloaf	35
Southwestern Sweet Potato Wedges	72
Spicy Chicken And Pepper Jack Cheese Bites	26
Spicy Sesame Tempeh Slaw With Peanut Dressing	63
Spinach & Brie Frittata	55
Spinach And Cheese Calzone	58
Spinach And Feta Stuffed Chicken Breasts	30
Sriracha Salmon Melt Sandwiches	48
Steak Fajitas	45
Street Corn	71
Sweet Potato Pie Rolls	87

T

Tandoori Paneer Naan Pizza	61
Tarragon Pork Tenderloin	42
Tex-mex Beef Carnitas	44
Tex-mex Potatoes With Avocado Dressing	62
Thai-style Pork Sliders	77
Thanksgiving Turkey Sandwiches	73
The Best Shrimp Risotto	49
Toasted Choco-nuts	70
Tomato & Squash Stuffed Mushrooms	55

Tortilla Crusted Chicken Breast	29
Truffle Vegetable Croquettes	66
Tuna Nuggets In Hoisin Sauce	47

V

Vanilla-strawberry Muffins	83
Vegan Brownie Bites	90
Vegetarian Eggplant "pizzas"	60
Vegetarian Paella	58
Veggie Fried Rice	63
Vodka Basil Muffins With Strawberries	19

W

White Bean Veggie Burgers	72
Wiener Schnitzel	43

Z

Zucchini Tamale Pie	62

Printed in Great Britain
by Amazon